Law & Liberty

R. J. Rushdoony

ROSS
HOUSE
BOOKS

Vallecito, California

Law & Liberty
by R.J. Rushdoony

Copyright 1984, 2009
Mark R. Rushdoony

Ross House Books
PO Box158
Vallecito, CA 95251
www.ChalcedonStore.com

All rights reserved.

Library of Congress: 2009906920
ISBN-10: 1-879998-55-6
ISBN-13: 978-1-879998-55-1

Other titles by
Rousas John Rushdoony

The Institutes of Biblical Law, Vol. I
The Institutes of Biblical Law, Vol. II, Law & Society
The Institutes of Biblical Law, Vol. III, The Intent of the Law
Systematic Theology (2 volumes)
Commentaries on the Pentateuch: Genesis,
Exodus, Leviticus, Numbers,
Deuteronomy
Chariots of Prophetic Fire
Sermon on the Mount
The Gospel of John
Romans & Galatians
Hebrews, James, & Jude
The Cure of Souls
Sovereignty
The Death of Meaning
Noble Savages
Larceny in the Heart
To Be As God
The Biblical Philosophy of History
The Mythology of Science
Thy Kingdom Come
Foundations of Social Order
This Independent Republic
The Nature of the American System
The "Atheism" of the Early Church
The Messianic Character of American Education
The Philosophy of the Christian Curriculum
Christianity and the State
Salvation and Godly Rule
God's Plan for Victory
Politics of Guilt and Pity
Roots of Reconstruction
The One and the Many
Revolt Against Maturity
By What Standard?

Chalcedon
PO Box 158 * Vallecito, CA 95251
www.ChalcedonStore.com

This volume is dedicated to
Dr. Ellsworth McIntyre
and the staff members of
Grace Community Schools, Naples, Florida
in great appreciation
for their generous support
of the work of my father.

Rev. Mark R. Rushdoony
President, Chalcedon Foundation

Contents

FOREWORD

These essays were delivered as a series of radio addresses in 1966 and 1967, over several stations from coast to coast. It would be wrong to say that they had a great popular reception, but, in all areas save one, the response was surprisingly good. These essays were written, not for broadcast, but for publication, as a summary statement of certain concepts of law and liberty.

Their radio broadcasting was in large part made possible by the underwriting of Mr. Paul R. Hackstedde of Arcadia, California, and their publication by the underwriting of Mr. Frederick Vreeland of Parsippany, New Jersey. Mrs. Arlene Gollnick of Orland, California, typed the manuscript. Mrs. Grayce Flanagan mimeographed copies of all these radio addresses for circulation. Mrs. Fleurette Edwards corrected the proofs, together with my wife Dorothy Rushdoony. I am very grateful to them for their help and for their concern for our common cause.

Rousas John Rushdoony

CAN WE LEGISLATE MORALITY?

An oft-quoted statement has it that we can't legislate morality. We are told that it is useless and even wrong to enact certain kinds of legislation because they involve trying to make people moral by law, and this, it is insisted, is an impossibility. Whenever various groups try to effect reforms, they are met with the words, "You can't legislate morality."

Now it must be granted that there is a measure of truth to this statement. If people could be made moral by law, it would be a simple matter for the board of supervisors or for Congress to pass laws making all Americans moral. This would be salvation by law. Men and nations have often resorted to salvation by law, but the only consequence has been greater problems and social chaos.

We can agree, therefore, that people cannot be *saved* by law, but it is one thing to try to *save* people by law, another to have moral legislation, that is, laws concerned with morality. The statement, "You can't legislate morality," is a dangerous half-truth and even a lie, because *all* legislation is concerned with morality. Every law on the statute books of every civil gov-

ernment is either an example of enacted morality or it is procedural thereto. Our laws are all moral laws, representing a
system of morality. Laws against manslaughter and murder
are moral laws; they echo the commandment, "Thou shalt
not kill." Laws against theft are commandments against
stealing. Slander and libel laws, perjury laws, enact the moral
requirement, "Thou shalt not bear false witness." Traffic laws
are moral laws also: their purpose is to protect life and property; again, they reflect the Ten Commandments. Laws concerning police and court procedures have a moral purpose
also, to further justice and to protect law and order. Every law
on the statute books is concerned with morality or with the
procedures for the enforcement of law, and all law is concerned with morality. We may disagree with the morality of a
law, but we cannot deny the moral concern of law. Law is concerned with right and wrong; it punishes and restrains evil
and protects the good, and this is exactly what morality is
about. It is impossible to have law without having morality
behind that law, because all law is simply enacted morality.

There are, however, different kinds of morality. Biblical
morality is one thing, and Buddhist, Hindu, and Moslem
morality radically different moral systems. Some moral laws
forbid the eating of meats as sinful, as for example, Hinduism,
and others declare that the killing of unbelievers can be a
virtue, as in Moslem morality. For Plato's morality, some acts
of perversion were noble forms of love, whereas for the Bible
the same acts are deserving of capital punishment.

The point is this: all law is enacted morality and presupposes a moral system, a moral law, *and* all morality presupposes a religion as its foundation. Law rests on morality, and
morality on religion. Whenever and wherever you weaken the
religious foundations of a country or people, you then weaken
the morality also, and you take away the foundations of its law.
The result is the progressive collapse of law and order, and the
breakdown of society.

This is what we are experiencing today. Law and order are
deteriorating, because the religious foundations, the Biblical

foundations, are being denied by the courts and by the people. Our American system of laws has rested on a Biblical foundation of law, on Biblical morality, and we are now denying that Biblical foundation for a humanistic one. From colonial days to the present, American law has represented Biblical faith and morality. Because it has been Biblical, our laws have not tried to *save* men by law, but they have sought to establish and maintain that system of law and order which is most conducive to godly society.

Now, our increasingly humanistic laws, courts, and legislators are giving us a new morality. They tell us, as they strike down laws resting upon Biblical foundations, that morality cannot be legislated, but what they offer is not only legislated morality but *salvation by law*, and no Christian can accept this. Wherever we look now, whether with respect to poverty, education, civil rights, human rights, peace, and all things else, we see laws passed designed to *save* man. Supposedly, these laws are going to give us a society free of prejudice, ignorance, disease, poverty, crime, war, and all other things considered to be evil. These legislative programs add up to one thing: *salvation by law*.

This brings us to the crucial difference between Biblical law and humanistic law. Laws grounded on the Bible do not attempt to save man or to usher in a brave new world, a great society, world peace, a poverty-free world, or any other such ideal. The purpose of Biblical law, and all laws grounded on a Biblical faith, is to punish and restrain evil, and to protect life and property, to provide justice for all people. It is *not* the purpose of the state and its law to change or reform men: this is a spiritual matter and a task for religion. Man can be changed only by the grace of God through the ministry of His word. Man cannot be changed by statist legislation; he cannot be legislated into a new character. The evil will or heart of a man can be restrained by law, in that a man can be afraid of the consequences of disobedience. We all slow down a bit on the freeway when we see a patrol car, and we are always mindful of speed regulations. The fact of law and the strict enforcement of law are restraints upon man's sinful inclinations. But, while a man can be *restrained* by strict law and order, he cannot be *changed* by law; he cannot be saved by law. Man can only be saved by the grace of God through Jesus Christ.

Now humanistic law has a different purpose. Humanistic law aims at saving man and remaking society. For humanism, salvation is an act of state. It is civil government which regenerates man and society and brings man into a paradise on earth. As a result, for the humanist social action is everything. Man must work to pass the right set of laws, because his salvation depends upon it. Any who oppose the humanist in his plan of salvation by law, salvation by acts of civil government, is by definition an evil man conspiring against the good of society. The majority of men in office today are intensely moral and religious men, deeply concerned with saving men by law. From the Biblical perspective, from the Christian perspective, their program is immoral and ungodly, but these men are, from their humanistic perspective, not only men of great dedication but men of earnestly humanistic faith and morality.

As a result, our basic problem today is that we have two religions in conflict, humanism and Christianity, each with its own morality and the laws of that morality. When the humanist tells us therefore that "You can't legislate morality," what he actually means is that we must not legislate Biblical morality, because he means to have humanistic morality legislated. The Bible is religiously barred from the schools, because the schools have another established religion, humanism. The courts will not recognize Christianity as the common law foundation of American life and civil government, because the courts have already established humanism as the religious foundation of American life. For humanism *is* a religion, even though it does not believe in God. It is not necessary for a religion to believe in God to be a religion; as a matter of fact, most of the world's religions are essentially humanistic and anti-theistic.

The new America taking shape around us is a very religious America, but its religion is humanism, not Christianity. It is a very morally minded America, but its ethics is the new morality, which for Christianity is simply the old sin. This new, revolutionary, humanistic America is also very missionary-minded. Humanism believes in salvation by works of law, and, as a result, we are trying, as a nation, to save the world by law. By vast appropriations of money and dedicated labor, we are trying to save all nations and races, all men from all problems, in the hopes of creating a paradise on earth. We are trying to bring peace on earth and good will among men by acts of state and works of law, not by Jesus Christ. But St. Paul wrote, in Galatians 2:16, "Knowing that a man is not justified by the works of the law, but by the faith of Jesus Christ, even we have believed in Jesus Christ, that we might be justified by the faith of Christ, and not by works of the law: for by the works of the law shall no flesh be justified."

Law is good, proper, and essential in its place, but law can save no man, nor can law remake man and society. The basic function of law is *to restrain* (Rom. 13:1-4), not to regenerate, and when the function of law is changed from the restraint of evil to the regeneration and reformation of man and society, then law itself begins to break down, because an impossible burden is being placed upon it. Today, because too much is expected from law, we get less and less results from law, because law is put to improper uses. Only as we return to a Biblical foundation for law shall we again have a return to justice and order under law. "Except the LORD build the house, they labour in vain that build it" (Ps. 127:1).

THE SANCTITY OF LIFE

One of the more prominent thinkers of this century, and a famous humanist, was Dr. Albert Schweitzer. By his own statements, Schweitzer was religiously not a Christian but a humanitarian. His basic religious principle was not Jesus Christ but *reverence for life*. For Schweitzer, reverence for life meant that all life is equally sacred and holy, and equally to be reverenced. The life of man and the life of a worm or a mosquito, the life of a saint and the life of the most depraved criminal, are equally sacred and equally to be revered. Any killing, even of plants and animals for food, is a guilty act of murder, so that man lives by guilt only. There can be no moral discrimination between men or between living things, because all equally represent *life*, and all life is sacred and holy. In varying degrees, this belief is widespread in our times. Many hold that capital punishment is murder, a crime against life, and that all warfare is murder and therefore totally to be condemned. Moreover, the new morality refuses to distinguish between moral and immoral acts in the Biblical sense: all acts are held to be moral which do no violence to life. Life is holy, and there can be no discrimination against any act which is an aspect of life.

People who hold to this faith are almost always pacifists, although some will justify the killing of fascistic enemies of humanity; they are against capital punishment, and they are against Christian morality because they claim it is restrictive of or hostile to life and the will to live.

To cope with this very prevalent faith, it is necessary to know the Biblical perspective thoroughly. The plain statement of the Ten Commandments is "Thou shalt not kill." The meaning of this commandment is that God as Creator is Lord over life and death: "See now that I, even I, am he, and there is no god with me: I kill, and I make alive; I wound, and I heal: neither is there any that can deliver out of my hand" (Deut. 32:39). Life is the gift of God; it must therefore be lived on His terms and according to His law. Man cannot take life, including his own, according to his own wishes without being guilty of murder. In many states, our law still reflects the Christian belief that attempted suicide is attempted murder and a criminal offense. Our life is not our own: we can neither live nor die according to our will but only according to God's will and word. As a result, the death sentence against murder is repeatedly pronounced in the Bible: "Whoso sheddeth man's blood, by man shall his blood be shed" (Gen. 9:6). "He that smiteth a man, so that he die, shall be surely put to death" (Ex. 21:12). "The murderer shall surely be put to death" (Num. 35:16-18). Murder, thus, is one of the crimes that calls for capital punishment.

But, some have argued, how can the Bible logically ask us to impose death as a penalty when it also forbids us to kill? The answer is a simple one. The right to kill does not belong to man; it belongs to God as the author of life. Life can be taken, capital punishment imposed, *only* according to the law of God and under commission from Him. Repeatedly the Bible tells us, as for example, in Romans 13:1-6, that officers of state, civil government officials, are ministers of God. Just as the church represents a ministry of the word and of the sacraments, and of church discipline, so the state or civil government represents a ministry, the ministry of justice, the administration of law and order under God. Moreover, just as the officers or ministers of the church must believe in and be faithful to God, or else incur His wrath and judgment, so also must the officers or ministers of the state believe in and be faithful to God, or else incur His wrath and judgment.

Because the officers of state exercise God's power, that is, the ministry of justice, with the power and right to take life, they are spoken of by God as "elohim" in Psalm 82, that is, as gods. They are like gods in that they share in God's authority over human life: to them is delegated the duty of killing men when men violate God's laws. When they discharge this duty according to God's word, their judgment is regarded as "judgments of God." According to Deuteronomy 1:17, in its instructions to civil officers and judges, "Ye shall not respect persons in judgment; but ye shall hear the small as well as the great; ye shall not be afraid of the face of man; for the judgment is God's." If the judges and officers of civil government fail to keep God's laws, if they pervert God's justice, then, according to Psalm 82, although their authority is like the authority of a god, they "shall die like men" (Ps. 82:7). God Himself will bring judgment and capital punishment on a country that despises His law.

As a result, from the Christian perspective capital punishment is not an option of the state, not a matter where civil government has a choice. The state has an ironclad law, the law of God, which it must obey, because the execution of criminals who incur the death penalty is required of the state at the penalty of the state's own life if it disobeys.

The rights of the criminal *are* protected by Biblical law. The legal principle that a man is innocent before the court until proven guilty is derived from the Bible. The same is true of the requirement of corroboration before a testimony is allowed to stand against a man. But the Bible makes clear that man proven guilty cannot be the object of pity. As Solomon summarized it, "They that forsake the law praise the wicked: but such as keep the law contend with them" (Prov. 28:4). Those who are full of pity for the guilty criminal are themselves men who have forsaken the law. Their pity for the criminal is itself a sign of depravity.

A few years ago, the father of a six-year-old girl who was brutally slain by a sex pervert, said, "I can't blame the man as much as the society which produced him." The criminal was clearly a degenerate man. But we must insist that this father himself was fearfully degenerate. This father was denying the doctrine of personal moral responsibility. He was turning the whole moral world upside down by calling the criminal the victim. He was despising God's law in favor of various sociological excuses for criminality. Solomon expressed clearly the consequences of such moral delinquency: "He that turneth away his ear from hearing the law, even his prayer shall be an abomination" (Prov. 28:9).

The power to kill thus is God's power; it must be exercised according to God's law, and it is not man's power but God's power. This godly use of the power to kill is, according to the Bible, also involved in just warfare.

But this is only one side of the matter. The power to kill is under God's law, and life and living are also under God's law. Nowadays, it is popular to think of laws as a restraint on life, and this is an attitude widely encouraged by existentialist humanism. The free life is the life beyond law, beyond good and evil, we are told; it is emancipation from law and morality. Our historic American position, however, has been the Christian faith that true liberty is under law, God's law. Godly wisdom, which means faith and obedience, is, according to Scripture "a tree of life to them that lay hold upon her" (Prov. 3:18; cf. 11:30). According to the Berkeley version of Psalm 19:7, "The law of the LORD is perfect, restoring the soul." Instead of being a form of bondage, God's law is for us the condition of life.

Let us analyze the meaning of this, God's law as the condition of life. The condition of a fish's life, its environment, is water; take a fish out of water, and it dies. The condition of a tree's life, its health and its environment, is the soil; uproot a tree, and you kill it. It is no act of liberation to take a fish out of water, or a tree out of the ground. Similarly, the condition of a man's life, the ground of man's moral, spiritual, and physical health, is the law of God. To take men and societies out of the world of God's law is to sentence them to a decline, fall, and death. Instead of liberation, it is execution. Man's liberty is under God's law, and God's law is the life-giving air of man and society, the basic condition of their existence. When Moses summoned Israel to obey God's law and to walk by faith, he said, "I call heaven and earth to record this day against you, that I have set before you life and death, blessing and cursing: therefore choose life, that both thou and thy seed may live" (Deut. 30:19). "Therefore choose life," and choosing life means living in obedience to God's law through faith in Jesus Christ, whose saving grace enables us to believe and obey.

Law is therefore the condition of man's life because God is the creator of life and the sole ground of its continuation. God's law is the essence of life and the terms of life. Those who tamper with God's law, or who espouse any departure from it, instead of seeking freedom to live, as they claim, are in actuality seeking death. For a fish, "escape" from water is an escape from life; it is a will to death. Jesus Christ, speaking as Wisdom ages ago, declared, "But he that sinneth against me wrongeth his own soul: all they that hate me love death" (Prov. 8:36). The hatred of God's law is the hatred of life: it is the love of death.

True government is government according to God's word, in terms of His law, as a ministry of justice. Those who despise government are, according to Moses (Num. 15:29-31) and St. Peter (2 Pet. 2:10), guilty of the sin of presumption. Presumption means taking for oneself authority and power for which one has no warrant or right. Whenever we set aside God's laws concerning life and death, we are guilty of presumption. Presumption is the mark of an unbeliever. Presumption means that we have set ourselves in the place of God and have demanded that life and death be on our terms only.

The presumptuous humanists talk about reverence for life, but, instead of having any regard for the sanctity of life, their view of life is secular and profane. Life for them has no connection with God; it is simply a natural resource to exploit and re-shape to their own tastes. They are presumptuous, that is, self-willed; their universe is essentially their own ego and their own intellectual pride, their confidence that they represent the elite ruling class of the ages. Their presumption makes them not only contemptuous of God but of other men. We live in a day when the love of all men is insistently proclaimed in theory, and massive hatred of all men is practiced in fact. We hear much about equality from men who tell us they are our superiors and therefore know what is best for us. We hear calls for unity from men whose every action divides us. Presumptuous men, because they are self-willed, can bring only anarchy. Faith and obedience bring unity because they unite men in Christ, not in man's will. "Except the LORD build the house, they labour in vain that build it" (Ps. 127:1).

THREE

LIBERTY: LIMITED OR UNLIMITED?

The issue of legislation governing pornography is becoming a major debate on the American scene. Shall legislation be further framed to abolish pornography, or does such legislation become censorship and a violation of civil rights?

Before analyzing the issue, let us examine the arguments for and against. In California, for example, the CLEAN Initiative, in 1966 Proposition 16 on the ballot, was one campaign among many to combat pornography. The advocates of CLEAN called attention to the fact that pornography in the United States has been a two billion dollar business annually. The publishers of pornography openly solicit manuscripts emphasizing perversions and hard-core pornography. Prosecution of avowedly pornographic works is difficult or impossible because existing laws are too weak. District attorneys do not initiate prosecutions, because the present law is inadequate to secure convictions. It is held that, to combat both pornography and its products, criminality and venereal disease, new laws are necessary.

Not so, the opponents argued. There is no necessary connection, it is claimed, between pornography and criminality,
between pornography and immorality. Moreover, even if it
were proven that such a connection exists, it would be wrong
to pass laws against pornography, because such laws would
introduce a greater evil, censorship and the loss of liberty. We
are told that if pornography is the price we must pay for liberty, then we must be prepared to pay it. Liberty is too basic to
the life of man to be sacrificed for any other factor. A lesser
good cannot be sacrificed for the greater and basic good. We
are against pornography, many argue, but we are even more
emphatically against censorship and against any and every
attack on liberty.

We can, as we assess these two conflicting positions, appre-
ciate both a concern for moral standards and also a concern
for liberty. The argument concerned with liberty is an important one, but it must be intelligently used. And what is liberty?
Can it be limited, or is true liberty only unlimited liberty?

Liberty is defined by the dictionary as "The state of being
exempt from the domination of others or from restricting circumstances." But this definition, like all others, presents problems. After all, who is free from the domination of others, and
free from restricting circumstances? We all have some domination to face: a husband, even a wife, parents, employers,
superior officers, tax collectors, the various forms of government, and so on. And, supremely, we are all under the
dominion and domination of God. And who is ever exempt
from restricting circumstances? After all, your income is a
restriction on your liberty: you can spend so much and no
more. Having a family is a restricting circumstance: it defini-
tively limits your liberty. The necessity of working is also a
restriction on our liberty, as is every other circumstance in our
life. Thus, according to this definition, only God is absolutely
free, because only God is "exempt from the domination of
others and from restricting circumstances." If we look to other
dictionary definitions, we are not much better off. Another
reads that liberty is "The power of voluntary choice; freedom

from necessity." But who is ever free from necessity in this life? The point, I think, is clear: no such thing as absolute or unlimited liberty is possible or good.

More than that, unlimited liberty for man is destructive of liberty itself. Can we give any man the unlimited liberty to do as he pleases? Can a man rob whenever he sees fit, kill at will, lie as he wishes, and generally be a law unto himself? If we permitted this, soon no one would have any liberty. The result would be only *anarchy*. Man's total liberty is always anarchy, and anarchy is the death of both law and liberty. Unless every man's liberty is limited by law, no liberty is possible for any man. The criminal law and the civil law impose mutual limitations on all of us in order to provide the maximum liberty for all of us.

As a result, we must be aware of those who talk about defending liberty when they actually want to promote anarchy. When we are told that there can be no laws against pornography without endangering liberty, we must challenge their claim to be interested in liberty. There is *no* area where freedom is unlimited. Take freedom of speech, for example: no man has a right to slander others, nor do our laws allow him the liberty to do so at will. Neither do we allow any man the liberty to shout "fire!" in a crowded theater when there is no fire. Freedom of speech does not give any man the right to walk onto the floor of Congress and speak his mind. His liberty is limited not only as to where he can say it but also as to what he says. This does not mean that I lack freedom to speak my mind, if it be done decently and in order.

Freedom of press means the liberty to publish, but it does not mean liberty to publish libelous statements, nor does it mean that any man can demand that his freedom of press be subsidized to enable him to publish. A man has the liberty to publish if he provides the cost of publication or interests a publisher in doing so. Moreover, the contents of what is published are also subject to limitations. Libel has already been cited. No man has the right, or liberty to publish another man's property, to publish stolen or copyrighted material. Again, no man has the right or liberty to publish materials violating the privacy of others. There are all kinds of legitimate and necessary restrictions on every kind of liberty man has, and these are necessary for the maintenance of liberty, because liberty cannot be equated with anarchy.

One of the necessary limitations on liberty is the suppression of pornography. Certainly mistakes have sometimes been made here, but they have also been made with reference to laws governing libel, privacy, slander, treason, crime, and every limitation on liberty. Neither man nor his laws are perfect, nor will they ever be in this life. The alternative to perfection is not anarchy; it is a realistic and working use of laws to further both human liberty and law.

One of the basic premises of the American system, and a basic article of Christian faith, is that man's liberty is under law. The purpose of law in the United States, has, historically, been to further liberty by law. Basic to all moral anarchism is the insistence that liberty can be gained only by *freedom from law*. From the beatniks and hippies to the student left and civil disobedience agitators, this belief in liberty as freedom from law runs deep. To prove that they are free, these immature and perverse minds insist on breaking some laws to demonstrate that they are free men. But moral anarchy is always the prelude to statist tyranny, and this vaunted *freedom from law ends always in a freedom from liberty!*

Liberty, then, is under law and it requires careful and conscientious legislation to maintain the social structure in that state of law which best promotes liberty. Limited liberty is the only kind of liberty possible to man. To dream of more is to endanger liberty itself.

The Rev. John Cotton, Puritan divine, wrote in the earliest days of New England, "It is necessary that all power on earth be limited." This premise became basic to all colonial government and to the United States. The restoration of true liberty requires the restoration of true law. It is a dangerous and totally false idea that freedom means an escape from law; this can be true only if the escape is from some such system as communism, and communism is not true law but *tyranny*.

To oppose in the name of liberty legislation against pornography is thus to favor anarchy rather than liberty. The basic premise of American law calls for liberty of speech and freedom of press, subject to the necessary restrictions of law and order. The purpose of current legislation proposals concerning pornography is *not* the destruction of liberty but its furtherance. It is a destruction of the freedom of press if libel is made legal, if stealing copyrighted materials is made permissible, and if violations of privacy are left ungoverned. The press then becomes a tyrant and a menace; it is out of control; it can invade your home, steal your writings, and also lie about you.

Pornography similarly is destructive of social order and of liberty. It is an insistence on the so-called right of moral anarchy, and, since its basic premise is anarchy, it brings anarchy also to every realm. *Liberty goes hand-in-hand with responsibility. The laws limiting freedom of speech and freedom of press are laws requiring responsibility.* Responsibility and liberty reinforce and strengthen each other. But pornography demands a world of moral anarchy, a world in which anything and everything goes, especially if it is perverted. As a matter of plain fact, the pornographer is hostile to law and order and to Christian morality. Being committed to moral anarchy, this is necessarily so. Being irresponsible, he is at war with the world of moral responsibility.

The defense of pornography on the ground of liberty, of freedom of press, is a false one, because the essence of pornography is dedicated moral irresponsibility, and this moral anarchism is an enemy of liberty under law. *Pornography denies the very concept of law;* it believes in a world without law and is dedicated to creating it. It must destroy liberty under law in order to usher in anarchy and a world without law.

The defense of our historic American system of liberty under law requires then that we wage war against pornography, because pornography is a major enemy to liberty.

The opponents of pornography are therefore no threat to liberty. Rather, they are its friends and defenders. Under the cloak and name of liberty, the pornographers are out to destroy liberty. The real champions of liberty are in every age hostile to pornography.

FOUR

THE POLITICS
OF PORNOGRAPHY

In order to understand some of the major currents of our day, it is necessary to recognize that one of the central purposes of pornography is political. An analysis of the politics of pornography is therefore essential.

Before doing so, it is necessary to call attention to a distinction made between pornography and obscenity. The novelist, Henry Miller, has said, "Obscenity is a cleansing process, whereas pornography only adds to the murk...Wherever a taboo is broken, something good happens, something revitalizing." Miller is by his own statement a champion of obscenity, but hostile to pornography. What is the distinction, if there is one? Basically, Miller's distinction is this: pornography is dirt for dirt's sake, whereas obscenity has as its purpose the systematic destruction of law and moral order, a revolutionary reordering of society. This distinction is only partially true. Obscenity does have this revolutionary purpose, consciously and openly. Pornography is more exploitive, but it has nonetheless an implicit or explicit revolutionary purpose. It is hostile to morality and law, and it encourages and favors rebellion against morality. As a result, it has political implications no less than Millers' obscenity. In discussing the politics of pornography, we are therefore analyzing the basic position of the whole field, pornography and obscenity. While there are differences in emphasis, the essential position is the same.

Now the *first* thing which is apparent in pornography is its obvious hatred of morality, its marked distaste for Biblical faith and morals. Moral restraint is seen as bondage for man, a slavery which must be destroyed. As a result, pornography indulges endlessly in long, tasteless, and highly emotional attacks on morality, on the sanctity of marriage, on monogamy, and on every kind of moral inhibition. It seeks to fan the flames of moral rebellion, to see morality as dull and restrictive, and immorality and perversion as exciting and liberating. Although people will attempt to prove almost anything these days it would be an impossibility to prove that pornography is not hostile to Biblical faith and morality, because it so obviously reeks with hatred and hostility.

A *second* observation is equally obvious: pornography sees a tremendous appeal in moral evil. Morality is seen as tedious and confining, as utterly boring and restrictive, whereas evil is portrayed as man's liberation. Evil has the potency of a magnetic force for the pornographer. The vitality, potency, and possibility of life are wrapped up in evil. Truly to live means for him evil, a commitment to and an involvement in moral evil. Man is not really alive, we are told, if he lives morally; life means evil; it means what is called sin and perversion. Only the person who sins is truly alive, it is held. Evil, for these people, is *life.*

Third, it can be further stated that for the pornographer *morality is death.* To confine men and women to the prison house of morality, marriage, law, and order is seen as equivalent to a sentence of death. Since evil is life, morality is logically death, and this is the religious faith of pornography. The gospel for man is thus evil; sin is the way of salvation, and the way to life and liberty. This faith is insistently presented, and with a religious fervor, and with good reason, because its roots are in an ancient religious faith, Manichaeanism, and also in various cults of chaos. For this faith, sin is life. Researchers a few years ago found that many people commit adultery, not because of any desire for the other person, but because of a fear that they will miss out on life if they do not sin. This is in essence the position of pornography—it offers sin and evil, and it declares it to be true life precisely because it is sin and evil.

Fourth, pornography manifests a hostility to the very idea of law and morality. Law means for it something inhibiting and stultifying, a deadening restraint upon man. Morality is held to be the dead hand of the past, the fearful and death-oriented will of men bound to superstition and fear. The destiny of man is to be free from law, according to these men, and the way to be free is to begin by breaking the law, by violating morality. Man's freedom is to be free from law, free to do as one pleases, and the mark of this freedom is the deliberate violation of all law and order. Very briefly, this position is one of moral anarchism. Man's greatest enemy is religion, morality, and law. Eliminate religious and moral law, and all the evils of human life will disappear. Man and the state can then reconstruct society in terms of man's liberation from God and create a truly human order, the great society of humanism, the city of man.

At the Second Annual Conference of Socialist Scholars, one of the leading lecturers called for "the collective worker in a collective society" and for "the destruction of monogamic bourgeois family as we know it" and for "complete freedom of sexual life."[1] In other words, man's freedom, he stated, involves being "exempt from worship" as well as morality, but man's freedom also involves a Marxist state! Slavery is religion and morality, and freedom is Marxist socialism. *Moral anarchism is the tool and instrument of totalitarianism, of socialism, and dictatorship.* Moral anarchism is used to destroy every form of social stability and order in order to pave the way for totalitarian order. Christianity gives to man the faith and character for self-government, and morality is the essence of self-discipline and self-

---

1. *Human Events,* September 24, 1966, 5.

government. Dissolve man's self-government and you make a totalitarian authority over him a social necessity. It becomes apparent, therefore, that the link between pornography and revolutionary totalitarianism is a necessary one. The rise of totalitarianism has always been preceded by moral anarchism, and those seeking tyrannical powers over man have always worked to reduce man to a dependent position by undercutting his moral self-government and responsibility. The rise and triumph of pornography is a prelude to totalitarianism. Moral anarchy is the seedbed of tyranny.

This then explains the relationship between pornography and totalitarianism. The champions of pornography talk loudly about liberty. Any legislation against pornography is protested as hostile to freedom of press and civil rights generally, but these same people are curiously silent about protesting the inroads of totalitarianism, of Marxism, into the social order. If they are interested in liberty, why not defend it against Marxism? The answer is that they are hostile to liberty; hence their defense of pornography is an instrument whereby man's moral liberty can be eroded and destroyed.

Our *sixth* point is thus an obvious conclusion: the politics of pornography is a moral anarchism whose purpose is revolution, a revolution against Christian civilization. The dean of modern pornographers and a great revolutionist was the Marquis de Sade. The Marquis called for total freedom for every kind of sexual perversion. For Sade, "true wisdom" meant "not...repressing...our vice...since these vices constitute almost the only happiness in our lives...to repress them would be to become our executioners." The Marquis called for the abolition of the death penalty, laws against theft, laws against murder, prostitution, adultery, incest, rape, sodomy, and all else. Equality required that all acts have equal standing before the law, except, of course, Christian moral laws such as monogamy, laws protecting property, and similar legislations. For Sade, Christianity and its moral laws should be abolished by law; all things else should be accepted. He defended all kinds of crimes and perversions as natural and good. "Can we possibly imagine Nature giving us the possibility of committing a crime which could offend her?...The most independent of men and those closest to Nature are savages; with impunity they devote themselves to murder every day."

The Marquis de Sade wrote with honesty. In his books, the politics of pornography is open and obvious. The contemporary pornographers are less open about stating their revolutionary goals, but they are still very obvious. The politics of pornography is simply the politics of revolution.

The sexual aspect of pornography is the most obvious aspect. It is an excellent come-on for the stupid and immature, but the underlying purpose is far more extensive in scope. It is nothing less than revolution. It is the reordering of life and society in terms of moral anarchism.

In *Esquire,* June, 1963, Anthony Lewis wrote on "Sex – and the Supreme Court," stating that after the Supreme Court's Roth decision, "no serious literary work can now be termed constitutionally obscene." All that a pornographer needs to do, if this be true, is to call attention to his serious purpose, namely, his revolutionary purpose, to seek to escape from prosecution. The "serious" purpose can be called sexual reform. Thus, in *The New Leader* for September 2, 1963, Stanley Edgar Hyman, writing on "In Defense of Pornography," wrote, "These books may teach and encourage a wider range of heterosexual activity, oral and anal as well as genital, and should be welcomed if they do." In other words, the increasing defense of pornography is that pornography itself is a socially redeeming activity and is therefore its own justification. In short, the plea for pornography is becoming the fact that it is pornography.

Many things can be said at this point. Certainly new and clearer legislation is necessary and urgently needed. Moreover, it is necessary that we recognize the radical and political implications of pornography. These things and more need to be done.

But positive actions must also accompany them—the reordering of life and society in terms of Biblical faith and standards. The basic answer to moral anarchism is the strengthening of Christian moral discipline. We need and must have sound legislations, but we must also establish the right kind of theological and moral foundations. If the foundations are destroyed, the structure will not stand. "Except the LORD build the house, they labour in vain that build it" (Ps. 127:1).

LAW AND NATURE

It has been so customary for men in Western civilization to think in recent centuries of natural law that it comes as a shock to some to hear doubts concerning it. But not every aspect of Western thought has always agreed that there is such a thing as natural law, nor have other cultures assented to it either. Thus a Chinese poet in the fifth century A.D. (Pao Chao, *The Ruined City*, 414-466) surveyed the past and present with a melancholy regret at the perversity of nature and history, concluding,

> The greatest displeasure of the largest number
> Is the law of nature.

Oriental philosophy has on the whole been skeptical and pessimistic about both nature and the supernatural. Its perspective has been one of either a basic agnosticism or atheism, and it has usually believed that nothingness is the ultimate truth about all things.

By contrast, originating in ancient Greek thought, Western thinkers have often believed in natural law. They have insisted that there is a higher law in nature as against the positive law of the state. In the late medieval period, especially from the Renaissance on, natural law philosophy came to dominate Western thinking until recently.

All this sounds academic and rather remote, but it is urgently relevant to our present problems. We cannot understand what has happened to our courts, especially the Supreme Court, without a knowledge of this problem, nor can we understand anything about our modern world situation without a grasp of it.

The problem in part is this. The advocates of natural law say that there is a higher law in nature which man's enlightened reason can discover. This higher law, which is inherent in nature, that is, it is in and of nature, is the true law by which men and nations must be governed.

Against this belief, two groups of thinkers are arrayed. *First*, there are the relativists, positivist, pragmatists, Marxists, existentialists, and others who deny natural law. For most of these thinkers, the only *real* law is *positive* law, the law of the state. There is no higher law or higher justice to pass judgment over man and the state. The only truth in being is human truth as it appears in history in the form of the state. As a result, men, instead of gearing their hopes to some nonexistent higher law, must gear their hopes to reality, and this means civil government, the state as man's hope.

Some years ago, this opinion, legal positivism, began to take over the United States Supreme Court. As we shall see, there were good grounds for this change. Central to this change in the court was Oliver Wendell Holmes, Jr., chief justice of the court and one of the most influential thinkers in its history. Everything that has since happened to the court is simply a product, a logical working-out, of Holmes's legal revolution.

Before criticizing Holmes, it is important to note that Holmes was very extensively on solid ground in criticizing natural law. The doctrine, he held, was simply legal nonsense, if not tyranny. Various rationalistic thinkers, governed by their concepts of logic, concluded that nature had inherent within it certain laws which were higher laws over man and the state. But the rationalism of these men varied, and as a result, their natural laws varied. Chinese, Hindu, Moslem, and Western legal thinkers and philosophers were by no means agreed as to what constitutes natural law. Those who held to natural law were, moreover, not agreed amongst themselves; their concepts of natural law varied in terms of their backgrounds, beliefs, and general cultural experience. Thus, experience, not a higher law or logic, was basic to law. As Holmes said, at the beginning of his study, *The Common Law* (1881), "The life of the law has not been logic: it has been experience. The felt necessities of the time, the prevalent moral and political theories, intuitions of public policy, avowed or unconscious, even the prejudices which judges share with their fellow men, have had a good deal more to do with the syllogism in determining the rules by which men should be governed ... The substance of the law at any given time pretty nearly corresponds, so far as it goes, with what is then understood to be convenient; but its form and machinery, and the degree to which it is able to work out desired results, depend very much upon its past." Holmes's statement is a very fair one: law has embodied experience, belief, and prejudice, and natural law is a law which is as variable as the persons expounding it. The question, of course, still remains as to whether a higher law lies in back of that experience. For Holmes, however, the rationalism of the natural law philosophers is a poorer guide than the experience of the people as embodied in the state. Holmes had no illusions about either, but he did prefer the broader basis of the experience of the people as embodied in the state.

More can be added in defense of Holmes's position. Darwinism dealt natural law a body blow. If evolution be true, then nature, instead of representing a perfect and final law order, is instead simply a blind, lawless force working its way upward and establishing its own rules, if they can be called that, by blind, unconscious experience. An *intelligent* experience, and an intelligent reflected experience, is known only by man. This intelligent reflected experience man uses to formulate law.

Law is therefore positive law, not a higher law. It is the experience of society embodied as the law of the state. It is therefore a changing, developing experience and law. Instead of being bound by a higher law or a past constitution, it must reflect present experience and reality. A constitution reflects dead experience, whereas man's present life is governed by living experience. The courts therefore must reflect the growing experiences of society intelligently and conscientiously, in order to ascertain the direction and form of these experiences.

Without agreeing with this position, it must be noted that there is much in its favor. If evolution be true, natural law is hopelessly dead, and legal positivism is a necessary conclusion for any modern thinker. The natural law thinkers begin on an Aristotelian or Enlightenment basis. They do not face realistically the implications of a post-Darwinian world. As a result, the courts, in choosing between these two positions, have simply kept up with the times. Intellectually, the Supreme Court justices have been especially alert to the philosophical currents of our day, and they have reflected with consistency what most people believe without consistency.

However, we stated that these legal positivists were one of two groups lined up against the old natural law concepts. The *second* group represents supernaturalism, Christian orthodoxy. According to these thinkers, whose presuppositions are governed by the Bible, laws *govern* nature, but these laws which *govern* nature are not therefore laws *of* nature but laws *over* nature. In other words, nature has no power, mind, consciousness, or will in and of itself. Nature is simply a collective noun, a name for the sum total of this universe. It is a collective noun, a name for the sum total of this universe. It is absurd to personify nature and to ascribe to it a law or purpose.

But this is not all. For the Christian thinker, nature cannot be normative, that is, it cannot be a standard. We cannot say, as moral anarchists do say, that a thing is good because it is natural, that is, because it occurs in nature. All kinds of things occur in nature—crimes, murders, thefts, perversions, and all manner of evils. According to Lenny Bruce, "Truth is 'what is.'" In other words, every kind of criminal activity is equally the truth with all things else, because it occurs in nature. The lie is that which tries to impose a standard of right and wrong in and over nature. There is for anarchism a total moral equality between all acts.

For the Christian, however, nature is not the standard, because the world of nature is a *fallen* world, a world in rebellion against God and infected by sin and death. For a standard, we must look beyond nature to God.

Now God has established various law spheres over nature, laws governing physical reality, laws governing society, morality, religion, the church, and all things else. In every area of our lives, we are governed by laws; whether we eat or sleep, work, worship, or play, we move in law spheres. Our eating obeys laws of nutrition and digestion; our sleep is governed by physiological laws; our every activity involves one law sphere after another. These law spheres are a part of God's creation; nature did not evolve them; they appeared together with nature when God created all things.

Our present legal crisis has its roots in Darwinism's demolition of natural law. The legal positivists believe that it is impossible to go back to the old eighteenth century belief in Nature as a kind of substitute for God, a Nature with hard and fast laws of its own making. Both reason and experience lead modern thinkers to agree substantially with the present Supreme Court. Law is the developing, intelligent, and reflected experience of the people of the state as expressed through the court.

But this makes the judges of the court into new gods of being—Plato's philosopher-kings who are the totalitarian rulers over mankind. Clearly, this is our present direction. The democratic consensus is best known, we are told, by the experts, who can best tell us what we should favor and believe. In short, when we deny God as our God, then we make men gods over us. The answer to natural law *and* to legal positivism is revelation. "Except the LORD build the house, they labour in vain that build it" (Ps. 127:1).

LAW AND THE FUTURE

Man is not alone in planning for the future. Animals store food, build nests, migrate to other climates, and, in a variety of ways, live in terms of tomorrow. With animals, however, such activity is instinctive. Man alone envisions a future, dreams of a hope or plan, and then works, self-consciously and purposefully, to realize that future.

Man lives, moreover, in terms of a future he believes in or looks forward to. To a very great degree, his life is governed and measured by his future. Recently, many very seriously ill hospital patients were questioned about their future. A high degree of correlation was found between thinking ahead and life expectancy. Those who could think ahead only a week usually lived a week; those whose vision included or spanned a month, lived a month. On the whole, it became apparent that usually, when a man's thinking has no future he has no life.

Historically, Western man's vision of the future has been Christian. Christian man has seen the future of history, and of himself personally, in terms of the triumph of Christ and the fulfillment of the Kingdom of God. Beginning in the seventeenth century, this Christian future was gradually replaced by a vision of history as the fulfillment of man apart from God, in terms of a religious and scientific humanism.

Utopian writing began to express this dream of a marvelous new world in which science and technology conquer all problems, and man becomes a new Adam, living in a new paradise on earth. For the Christian the basic problem and roadblock is *sin*; for the scientific utopian, the basic problem is *insufficient science and technology*. As science and technology develop, all man's problems will disappear.

In the Soviet Union especially, science fiction became the expression of this hope. Science cannot fail; technology will overcome all problems. The future will see communism triumph because it is scientific, and it avails itself of every instrument of science to create the perfect future for man. For Communist science fiction, there is no failure, only the steady triumph of scientific socialism. In the United States, many science fiction writers are beginning to see *sin* in man's future destroying or misusing all the powers opened up by science and technology to create a hell on earth. The result is a vision of the future filled with great horrors and no faith. The American perspective is half-humanistic; it sees science as a new god and able to create almost at will. But the American perspective is also half-Christian; it sees science as also subject to original sin and thus able to use its powers to unleash fearful calamities and destruction. The Soviet Communist is forbidden to doubt the future; it is a question of science and controls, not a question of religion. The American still sees the scientist producing science; he sees the men behind science and is distrustful of man. The American is ready to believe in sin and depravity but not in salvation.

Now law is also closely connected with our thinking about the future, and it is very closely connected with social planning. As a matter of fact, *law* is the basic form of social planning. God's law, His eternal decree, is His predestination of man and the universe, His foreordination and creation of the future. Man attempts to do the same thing with law, both under God and apart from Him. When the U.S. Constitution was written in 1787, that law was a plan for the future of the federal government under God. Because the framers did not claim omnipotence or perfection, they left room for improvements or corrections by means of amendments, but they did impose a basic law on the federal union as a plan for its future. The minutes of the Constitutional Convention give us their hopes and fears for the future, and they devised the Constitution as a means of realizing their hopes and preventing their fears from realization.

Thus, law is the basic form of social planning. Every law is geared to a belief concerning the nature of society; every law is expressive of some faith concerning life, liberty, and property, and it is a part of a plan to realize an envisioned future.

The question that we must ask therefore is simply this: *of what plan are our new laws a part?* They represent, as do all laws, a piece of social planning, but *what plan?*

As we analyze these new laws, certain facets become more and more clear. *First,* our laws are increasingly alien to Christian faith; they do not see man and the republic as "under God." Instead, they are clearly humanistic. As a result, we do face a major legal revolution, and it is already well under way. *Second,* for American law, from its earliest days to the present, sin has been the problem. Checks and balances, divisions of powers, express powers, criminal law, civil law, and various levels of civil government all were designed to cope with the fact that man is a sinner, and he is no less a sinner when he becomes a civil official but rather more potentially or ably a sinner. Increasingly, our legal revolution is geared to a denial of the doctrine of sin. Not sin but environment is at fault. The answer is a change of environment through legislation, and this changed environment will thereupon change man. Instead of Christian salvation, man needs scientific reconditioning, either through mental health programs, wars on poverty, master plans for areas and peoples, or by means of controls.

Third, for the new law, man's liberty is from God and from religion. The state must be separated from God, but it is not separated from agnosticism or atheism, and it embraces humanism. It affirms the sufficiency of man and the state apart from and without God. For the Christian, man's true liberty is under God and from sin, and from the tyranny of sin as it manifests itself in man, the church, and the state.

Fourth, for Christian law, the future is a godly and law-abiding society under God, free from the tyranny of men and free to realize itself under God. For humanistic law, social planning as realized in laws has as its goal a scientific, humanistic world in which an elite plan for and govern all men in terms of technology and reason.

In discussing science fiction, we saw that the Soviet Union has a determined goal in terms of scientific socialism, and it is governing all things in terms of achieving that goal. American science fiction reveals a schizophrenic vision of the future—a partial commitment to scientific, socialistic humanism, and a partial retention of the Christian faith that man's basic problem is sin and his basic answer is salvation through Jesus Christ.

Because of our ignorance of the Bible, of our Christian foundations, the erosion in our historic American system is both deep and widespread. Many of the people who are most worked up over this problem are the least prepared to cope with it, because they lack Christian foundations. They know the problem well. They can document our American crisis by the hour, with voluminous detail. But they are basically humanistic in spite of themselves because of their radical ignorance of the faith. It is not too difficult to stand by bedsides and know when men are dying, and to say so. It is much more difficult to prescribe the medicine, or perform the surgery necessary, to save a man's life.

Law is a plan for the future. To return to law which undergirds and establishes a Christian future under God, it is necessary to know God in Christ, and to know His law and to know it well. The future we want is a future under God, not under tyrants. The law we need is a law which protects the Christian man in his God-given liberties rather than a law giving the state god-like powers over man.

A humanistic law must find its god and its devil in the world of man, since it denies any supernatural realm. Thus, a very influential book, written in Russia just three years after the Revolution, Eugene Zamiatin's *We*, sees the future as a one-world order populated by people whose names are numbers. Every man has a "zip-code" instead of a name. The god of this world is named *We*, and its devil is *I*.

The thinking here is logical. If the supernatural is eliminated, then the natural must be the root and source of good and evil, the source of the god and the devil for the system. For the collectivist or socialist, the god is *We*; for the anarchist, the god is *I*. Both the *I* and the *We*, the individual and the group, become fearful monsters when they are made into gods, and, under humanism, one or the other must prevail. The loser becomes the devil and must be destroyed. This is why, under humanism, tyranny is inescapable. The very word *tyranny* comes from an ancient Greek word meaning "secular rule," that is, rule by man rather than by means of God's law. The true remedy for tyranny is not the rule of a church but of godly law, the rule of law which plans for a present and a future under the sovereignty of God. As the psalmist said long ago, "Except the LORD build the house, they labour in vain that build it" (Ps. 127:1).

LAW AND AUTHORITY

All thinking appeals to authority, and the question to ask of any man or of any philosophy or religion, is simply this: "What is its authority?" To what does it appeal as the foundation, the basis, of its thinking?

Now we are used today to hearing some express their contempt of all authority. In particular, many college radicals are quite vocal, as are many of their professors, in despising any appeal to authority. Supposedly, they are free minds and need no such appeal. But all such claims represent either hypocrisy or ignorance, because there is no possibility of any thinking without authority. The only question is which authority?

For many of these supposedly anti-authoritarian persons, their basic authority is *the individual.* In other words, they recognize no God or man as authoritative, and they exalt their own thinking to a position of ultimacy. They become gods in their own eyes. In essence, their faith is that every man should be his own god, but that no man can be free or become his own god unless he agrees with them. This position is essentially anarchism, and it is as intolerant and exclusive a kind of authoritarianism as any. The hostility of these anarchists is to every kind of authoritarianism except their own.

People who profess to be believers in democracy also have their own brand of authoritarianism. They claim that democracy is the true way of life and the true form of civil government because it rests on the true foundation, the people. The ancient faith in democracy is summed up in the Latin phrase, *vox populi, vox Dei,* the voice of the people is the voice of God. The people are thus the god of democracy. No law, no constitution, no religious faith can be permitted to stand in the way of the will of the people. The will of the people incarnates itself in a governing elite who express this general will infallibly. There is a direct connection between the democratic thinking of Rousseau and Karl Marx' dictatorship of the proletariat.

In any system of thought, authority is inescapable. In this respect, every religion, political faith, philosophy, and science is authoritarian. Each appeals to a basic and ultimate authority, to God or man, to the individual or to people in the mass, to reason or to experience; whatever the case may be, something is the underlying authority in every system of thought. Science is as authoritarian as any religion. Science rests on certain authoritative beliefs that undergird all science. Science holds, for example, to the faith, first, that reality is measurable. In other words, what is real is that which can be measured. Second, science holds that reality has unity, uniformity, so that knowledge of reality is possible because reality does not contradict itself. These and many other axioms or presuppositions of science are basically religious beliefs, and they provide the authority for science.

No man can escape the problem of authority. Every man will consciously or unconsciously appeal to some authority as basic and ultimate to life. Most authorities revered by men today are human authorities: the individual, the people, the elite thinkers and planners, science, reason, or the state, these are all humanistic authorities.

When a man's authorities are of this world, then man is in danger. These authorities are then not only ultimate, they are also proximate or present. They stand right over him with all their imposing claims, and, because they occupy the same ground man does, they limit and destroy the liberty of man.

Two things of the same world cannot occupy the same point in time and space. If a man's gods or authorities are of this world, they will insist on occupying *his* place in time and space, and the result is the enslavement and eviction of man from his due liberties and station in life. A man cannot compete with his authorities, with his gods; they are by his own recognition above and over him. If a man's gods are of this world, and if they are man-made and humanistic, they know only one realm to occupy, man's realm. This is why anarchism and democracy, while professing to exalt man, end by oppressing him. This, too, is why humanistic science, while claiming to serve man, ends by using man as its experimental test animal, its guinea pig.

The authority of any system of thought is the god of that system. Men, by denying God, cannot escape God. God is the inescapable reality, and the inescapable category of thought. When men deny the one true God, they do it only to make false gods.

Behind every system of law there is a god. To find the god in any system, locate the source of law in that system. If the source of law is the individual, then the individual is the god of that system. If the source of law is the people, or the dictatorship of the proletariat, then these things are the gods of those systems. If our source of law is a court, then the court is our god. If there is no higher law beyond man, then man is his own god, or else his creatures, the institutions he has made, have become his gods. When you choose your authority, you choose your god, and where you look for your law, there is your god.

The ground of liberty is Jesus Christ. Biblical faith places authority in the triune God—God the Father, God the Son, and God the Holy Ghost—and in God's inspired and infallible word, the Bible. God does not compete with man as humanistic authorities do. He is above, over, and beyond man. The purpose of His law and of His government is to establish man in godly order and in true liberty. Because God has created this world and history, God does not seek to obliterate history but to bring man and history to fulfillment.

Authority in Biblical faith is in this world only under God. Men are given authority over their wives, and parents over children, under God and subject to His laws. The authority of the state over its citizens and the authority of the church over its members are always subject to the prior authority of God and the supremacy of His law. In every area, God undergirds legitimate authority, which is His creation, by His word and law. But, in every area, God also limits all human authority by His own sovereignty and by His word. No human authority can claim to be ultimate, nor can any authority speak with final power.

Just as it is impossible for man to live without authority, so it is impossible for man to live without law. Moreover, every honest system of law will openly avow its basic authority and disavow every other authority. Every law presupposes a basic authority, and the ultimate authority of every system of thought is the god of that system.

It is apparent therefore that we are sadly astray today in our thinking about law. Our law has ceased to be Christian and has become humanistic and democratic. Its purpose is to establish the will of mass man, of democratic man, as the ultimate authority. As a result, our law is increasingly an anti-Christian system of law. It is hostile to the sovereignty of God, and it affirms the sovereignty of man. Our lawmakers are saying in effect, "Let us make god in our own image, after our likeness." They are bent not only on remaking law but on remaking man.

God's law has as its purpose the government of man, to guide and direct man into the way of righteousness and truth.

Grace recreates man, and law is the form of the new man's life, in that man is regenerated in order to be conformed to God.

Man's law seeks to remake man in terms of the humanistic state's plan for man. As a result, the humanistic state, as the new god over man, controls every fact of life in order to use all things to remake man. Education is increasingly used in order to teach statism and to mold the minds of children. The motto of progressive educators, "We do not teach subjects; we teach children," is very apt. Their purpose is not the communication of knowledge to children but to re-shape children to their ideas of democracy. The schools thus are instruments of social regeneration. Instead of rebirth by Jesus Christ, they offer rebirth by means of statist, progressivist curriculum. The public schools are the creatures of the state, and therefore they teach and exalt the authority of the democratic state. They exalt the authority of democracy and under-cut the authority of God, whom they bypass as though He were irrelevant to education. The public schools are thoroughly authoritarian and their authority is democracy.

Authority *is* inescapable. The basic question is *which authority*, the authority of God or of man? If we choose man, we have no right to complain against the rise of totalitarianism, the rise of tyranny—we have asked for it. If we choose God's authority, then we must submit to it without reservation; we must accept His infallible word and must in all things acknowledge His sovereignty. On this foundation, we are "founded upon the rock," Jesus Christ, and we shall not fall (Matt. 7:24-27).

LAW AND CHAOS

If we believe that the universe evolved out of a primeval chaos, we then hold chaos to be the primary and ultimate factor and force of the universe. Chaos is then the source and origin of all things and is the given, the datum, the undergirding force of the cosmos. Instead of God as the source, we then have chaos.

All non-Biblical religions trace their origins to chaos. Creation is seen, not as an act but a process, a growth, development, or evolution. Only in the Bible do we have creationism; every other religion rests on process-philosophy. In the religions of antiquity, the gods themselves are a product of process; they themselves are born of chaos.

Now, as I have shown in my study, *The Religion of Revolution,* when chaos is ultimate, when chaos is the source of all things, as it is in evolution, then regeneration is by means of chaos. Chaos is the formless, the completely disorderly, the absolutely lawless source of all things. As the source of all things, chaos is thus also the basic and underlying *energy* and *power* of the universe. Instead of deriving all power from God and His

creative act, evolution derives all energy and power from primeval chaos. Chaos is ultimate; hence, it is the basic force of
the universe.

In such an evolutionary perspective, regeneration—
rebirth—for man and for society is therefore by chaos. The
Christian goes to the triune God, revealed in Jesus Christ, to
be born again. All believers in evolutionary and process phi-
losophies go to chaos to be born again.

As a result, in all paganism the basic religious rite or festival
was a ritual of chaos, of which the Roman Saturnalia was one
form. During the festival of chaos, practices normally forbidden became religiously required. Incest, adultery, all forms
of perversion, all forms of lawlessness, became mandatory and
necessary and were practiced by all. It was belief in being born
again by means of chaos. Both to have personal rebirth and
social regeneration, chaos was necessary. Evolution is a
modern form of the cults of chaos, and the publication of
Darwin's *Origin of Species* was hailed with delight by Marx and
Engels. They saw immediately that it provided, as Marx wrote
to Lassalle, "a basis in natural science for the class struggle in
history" and for revolution. For communism, social regeneration is by means of chaos. Even when a country is taken over
peacefully, revolution must be applied to it from above. Revolution is planned chaos as regeneration. It is a religious principle. Both evolution and Marxism are modern forms of the
ancient cults of chaos.

Now Biblical faith is in creationism; not chaos but God is
ultimate. God has created all things, sustains all things, and
only God can recreate all things. Regeneration is by God's *grace*
through the atonement of Jesus Christ. Grace does not set aside
the law; it fulfills and establishes the law. As St. Paul declared in
Romans 3:31, "Do we then make void the law through faith?
God forbid: yea, we establish the law." The *purpose* of the law is
life. As St. Paul said, it "was ordained to life" but, because of sin,
"I found to be unto death" (Rom. 7:10). In itself, according to
Paul, "the law is holy, and the commandment holy, and just,
and good" (Rom. 7:12). "For we know that the law is spiritual:

but I am carnal, sold under sin" (Rom. 7:14). Man in Christ dies to the law as an indictment, a sentence of death, which Christ assumed for us. Man lives in Christ, not to despise God's law but now to abide by it through the grace of God. Grace is the believer's life, and law is its condition.

When man was created and established by God in the Garden of Eden, man was given the principle of law to live by. Genesis 2 makes this very clear. Paradise was not a lawless domain. On the contrary, the principle of law prevailed absolutely. Man had from the beginning the responsibility of moral choice with respect to the tree of the knowledge of good and evil. By his daily obedience, man said that God is the sovereign and the determiner of all things; God alone can declare what is good and what is evil, and man the creature must obey. The temptation of Satan was, "ye shall be as gods, knowing good and evil" (Gen. 3:5). Every man shall be his own god, determining what is good and evil for himself. Thus, *first* of all, the principle of law was at stake daily in Paradise. Would man recognize God as the source of law, or would man declare himself to be the source of law?

Second, law was involved in Adam's responsibility to care for Eden. Work, then, without the curse, was his responsibility to God, and the law of man's daily life involved accountability for his labor and a responsibility to discharge his duties. Work is a basic law sphere. Our attitude towards work is a part of our attitude towards law.

Third, man was under law in Paradise in that he was given the responsibility of naming the animals. Now *to name* in the Hebrew means to classify, to define the nature of, and a man's name in Old Testament times was also his definition. A man's name could therefore change several times in his life, as his life changed. Naming the animals was therefore a scientific task for Adam. It required understanding the basic laws of creation, of species and kinds, and classifying and identifying animals in terms of laws of their creation. Again, Adam was strictly bound to recognize and understand God's laws.

Fourth, law was paramount in Adam's marriage. Eve was not created simultaneously with Adam, but only after a considerable lapse of time, during which he had been active in his classification of nature and in his responsibility for Eden. Adam observed the male and female nature of animals but also saw that there was no helpmeet for him. In other words, Adam's marriage was not to be merely in fulfillment of biological law, but in terms of God's calling. Only as Adam found himself as a man in his vocation, in his responsibility, and in his understanding, was he then given Eve as his wife.

The principle of law, God's law, was thus paramount in Paradise. The image of God in man, in its narrower sense, is knowledge, righteousness, holiness, and dominion. The development and realization of that image was through law. When man fell, the salvation of man by the grace of God through the atoning work of Jesus Christ, reestablished man in communion with God. It placed man again in relationship to God, and the rules of man's relationship are law, God's law. As St. Paul said, "For this ye know, that no whoremonger, nor unclean person nor covetous man, who is an idolater, hath any inheritance in the kingdom of Christ and of God" (Eph. 5:5). We are not saved to despise the law but we are saved to keep the law as the righteousness of God.

Now the essence of any evolutionary perspective is its concept of change and development out of chaos. Thus, it both emphasizes *chaos* as the ultimate power, and *change* as the constant factor. If chaos is ultimate, then revolution is a necessary form of social regeneration. If change is the constant factor, then law is a changing factor, and we cannot have a belief in an absolute law, in an ultimate good and evil, in a constant right and wrong. Change is then the only law of life, and the means of change is chaos and revolution.

Our world today is caught in the forces of revolution and of change. The change is not growth, but change for the sake of change. Revolution only deepens our crisis, but men turn to revolution for salvation. In fact, for modern evolutionary thinking, *revolution is salvation.*

We cannot begin to combat these revolutionary forces unless we first of all challenge their evolutionary foundation. The myth of evolution, a modern form of an ancient cultural myth, must be challenged in the name of Biblical creationism, without any apology or hesitancy, and without any concessions. The creation of all things by God in six days is the plain statement of Scripture. It is the necessary premise, the foundation, of Biblical faith. For men to compromise and to substitute other foundations means to substitute man for God, and man's thinking for God's word, and the consequence can only be disaster. "Except the LORD build the house, they labour in vain that build it" (Ps. 127:1).

LAW AND EVOLUTION

How we define law depends greatly on what we believe. The definition of law therefore varies from religion to religion, culture to culture, and from philosophy to philosophy. Those who hold to the Christian faith see law as an ultimate order of the universe. It is the invariable factor in a variable world, the unchanging order in a changing universe. Law for the Christian is thus absolute, final, and an aspect of God's creation and a manifestation of His nature. In terms of this, the Christian can hold that right is right, and wrong is wrong, that good and evil are unchanging moral categories rather than relative terms.

From an evolutionary perspective, however, we have a very different concept of law. The universe is evolving, and the one constant factor is *change*. It is impossible therefore to speak of any absolute law. The universe has evolved by means of chance variations, and no law has any ultimacy or absolute truth. As a result, when we talk about law, we are talking about social customs or mores and about statistical averages. Social customs change, and what was law to the ancient Gauls is not law to the modern Frenchmen. We can expect men's ideas of law to change as their societies change and evolve. Moreover, statistics give us an average and a mean which determine normality, and our ideas of law are governed by what is customary and socially accepted.

For example, Emile Durkheim, in *The Rules of Sociological Method*, had a chapter "On the Normality of Crime." *First* of all, Durkheim saw crime as normal "because a society exempt from it is utterly impossible." Every society in every age has its criminals; therefore, crime is a part of normality. *Second*, since Durkheim believed in evolution rather than God, there was for him no law of God declaring crimes to be evil. The only thing against crime is social disapproval and condemnation, and this rests on the organization of society. If society were differently organized, these crimes might be regarded as desirable traits. *Third*, crime makes for progress, because it challenges authority, and according to Durkheim, "To make progress, individual originality must be able to express itself." The criminal thus breaks up the fixity of society from below so that the idealist above can find expression and freedom. The criminal is thus the ally of the social revolutionist.

Fourth, the criminal himself is a pioneer of evolution. As Durkheim said, "Where crime exists, collective sentiments are sufficiently flexible to take on a new form, and crime sometimes helps to determine the form they will take. How many times, indeed, it is only an anticipation of future morality—a step toward what will be!" Instead of being a parasite and an unsocial being, the criminal is thus for Durkheim an evolutionary pioneer. "Crime, for its part, must no longer be conceived as an evil that cannot be too much suppressed." Crime, then, must be given serious sociological attention: "If crime is not pathological at all, the object of punishment cannot be to cure it, and its true function must be sought elsewhere."

Fifth, Durkheim stated, "The various principles we have established up to the present are, then, closely interconnected. In order that sociology may be a true science of things, the generality of phenomena must be taken as the criterion of their normality." In other words, any criminal activity, as it becomes prevalent, becomes normal and acceptable. Instead of talking, then, about a breakdown of law and order, the evolutionist must logically talk about changing the law, because the current crimes and perversions are becoming the new law of society. Those who hold to the older morality are now the social deviates. A mother, herself a biologist, complained to me a few years ago that her son, finding the lawless nature of his classmates uncongenial, had withdrawn from his studies. The teacher's comment to the mother was that her boy was the "deviate." In terms of Durkheim's statistical standard, the teacher was right. In terms of this evolutionary standard, all who oppose departures from law, all who hold to an undeviating good and evil, are dubbed extremists and social deviates.

In terms of social evolution, man finds himself perpetually in the social self. Man must always be in tune with the social scene; he must be with it to be himself. Thus, Charles H. Cooley, in writing on "The Social Self,"[1] said that the individual, the "'I' is a militant social tendency, working to hold and enlarge its place in the general current of tendencies. So far as it can it waxes, as all life does. To think of it as apart from society is a palpable absurdity of which no one could be guilty who really *saw* it as a fact of life." Cooley then quoted Goethe, "Only in man does man know himself; life alone teaches each one what he is."[2] In other words, man is a product of social evolution; therefore, he cannot be defined in terms of God; he can be defined only in terms of the social scene. He is nothing in himself; man is only an aspect and part of society. To think of man as anything apart from society Cooley called "a palpable absurdity." Man then is simply a social animal, and he can only be known and defined in terms of his pack, society. In terms of this, man, instead of being created in the image of God, is created in the image of society. Man, instead

---

1. Charles H. Cooley, *The Two Major Works of Charles H. Cooley: Social Organization* and *Human Nature and the Social Order* (Glencoe: IL: The Free Press, 1956).
2. Ibid., Goethe, *Tasso*, Act 2, Sc.3.

of being governed by the law of God, is then accordingly governed by the law of the pack, the law of society in evolution. There is then no higher law: there is only the law of society as it evolves. What is right today may be wrong tomorrow. What is perversion today may be noble "platonic" love tomorrow. Law has no ultimate truth to it, no absolute morality undergirding it. It is simply social custom and the force of the state.

For Biblical faith, man is not a creature of social evolution but the creature of God, created in His image, with knowledge, righteousness, and holiness, and with dominion (Gen. 1:27-28; Col. 3:14; Eph. 4:24). Man is to be understood, therefore, not by reference to society, but by reference to God. The law of man's being is derived, not from society, but from God his Maker. God's law is the condition of man's life and its ground for health. As Moses said, "the Lord commanded us to do all these statutes … that he might preserve us alive" (Deut. 6:24). Again, "Justice, and only justice, you shall pursue, that you may live (Deut. 16:20, NAS). Instead of being judged socially, men and societies must be judged religiously, by the sovereign and triune God. But, for Auguste Comte, in his study, *The Positive Philosophy*, "social phenomena are subject to natural laws," that is, society is a product of biology and cannot transcend it. Man is not more than his biology.

If man is no more than biology, then man's law is no more than a phase of his social evolution and will change as man changes.

There is thus no absolute right and wrong in any evolutionary system of law, so that evolution is in essence hostile to the very idea of law. Law implies an unchanging order, a final standard, whereas evolution insists that law is social experience, custom, and mores. As a result, evolutionary thinking is unable to *formulate* a concept of law; it *uses* law as an instrument of social change. Evolutionary thinking makes law *relative* and *changing*, but the mechanism of change is thereby made *absolute*. Now the mechanism of evolution has been natural process, but is has become increasingly the scientific socialist state and its elite planners. When man is made controller of his own evolution by means of the state, the state is made into the new absolute. Hegel, in accepting social evolution, made the state the new god of being. The followers of Hegel in absolutizing the state are Marxists, Fabian, and other socialists, pragmatists, and virtually all modern schools of thought. In brief, God and His transcendental law are dropped in favor of a new god, the state. Evolution thus leads not only to revolution but to totalitarianism. Social evolutionary theory, as it came to focus in Hegel, made the state the new god of being. Biological evolutionary thinking, as it has developed since Darwin, has made revolution the great instrument of this new god and the means to establishment of this new god, the scientific socialist state.

The world therefore is committed to revolution because it is committed to evolution. The world is dedicated to change without meaning because it is governed by law without God. Crisis succeeds crisis, because revolutionary change is man's new idea of health, and, in every change, the state emerges more powerful and more clearly as man's new god and savior. There can be no withstanding this new god except by means of the only true God. "Except the LORD build the house, they labour in vain that build it" (Ps. 127:1).

LAW AND ALCHEMY

An important factor in history has been alchemy. Alchemy is a belief that the baser metals can be transmuted into gold, and that the processes of life can be reversed, so that aging can give way to youth. Its origins are in antiquity, going back at least to Babylon. According to alchemists, nature is in process of evolution and the goal of evolution is upwards. All the variations in nature are imperfections, failures, and experiments towards the realization of the best. Hence, in the world of metals, all metals other than gold are imperfections and abortions of nature, experiments that failed. Whether in the Near East, ancient China, Indo-China, India, or elsewhere, man in antiquity believed extensively in the natural metamorphous of metals.

The basis of this faith was evolutionary. Nature is in process of development, and the best in nature represents the present highest form of development and the potential of all other forms. The purpose of the alchemist was to speed up this natural, evolutionary process. Thus, a fourteenth-century work on alchemy, the *Summa Perfectionis*, stated that "what

Nature cannot perfect in a vast space of time, we can achieve in a short space of time by our art." In other words, the alchemist's science would by experimentation accomplish what normally millions of years were required to do. In his play, *The Alchemist*, Ben Johnson stated the same idea: "The egg's ordained by Nature to that end and is a chicken in potential ... The same we say of lead and other metals, which would be gold, if they had the time ... And that our art doth further" (Act II, sc. 2). Similarly, death is seen as a failure which evolution will some day overcome, as it will also overcome aging, and so the alchemist dedicated himself also to speeding up evolution to produce the youthful and immortal man as the new god over creation.

The alchemist depended in part on a return to the beginning, to chaos, to create the forward thrust of evolution. Mircea Eliade, in *The Forge and the Crucible*, quotes an old Taoist-Zen document to illustrate this point: "By returning to the base, the origin, we drive away old age, we return to the condition of the foetus." Eliade comments, "Now this 'return to the beginning,' as we have just seen, was what the alchemist also sought by other means." In other words, evolution requires chaos, revolution, to effect regeneration. The purpose of the alchemist was to create the conditions of chaos in order to further the leap ahead in evolution. It is not at all surprising therefore, that in the Enlightenment alchemists were closely allied to and central in the forces of revolution. *Revolution is simply the theory of social alchemy.* According to Paracelsus, the world must "enter into its mother," that is, into chaos, into the abyss, in order to achieve eternity. The alchemists talked about being born again, as occultists do today, but they meant by it the return to chaos as the means of regeneration.

There are strong elements of alchemy in psychoanalysis. By means of analysis, the patient is regressed into the primitive, anarchic unconscious and is supposedly thereby released from bondage and socially revitalized.

In order to be an alchemist, it was necessary to negate the present order in the name of primeval chaos. This meant denying law and order as sterile and finding power in chaos. Basil Valentine said, "Evil must become the same as good" for the adept. Perfect knowledge meant denying all present values in favor of the power of chaos to create a new order.

The purpose of the alchemist was thus to further evolution by acting as the agent of evolution. In Eliade's words, "One common factor emerges from all these tentative probings: in taking upon himself the responsibility of changing Nature, man put himself in the place of Time; that which would have required millennia or aeons to 'ripen' in the depths of the earth, the metallurgist and alchemist claim to be able to achieve in a few weeks." Eliade states further that the tools and equipment of the alchemist, "his furnaces, his retorts, play an even more ambitious role. These pieces of apparatus are at the very centre of a return to primordial chaos, of a rehearsal of cosmogony."

Thus, alchemy is the metamorphosis, the transmutation, the change of man and his world by means of chaos; man speeds up his own evolution by recreating the original chaos of being. Revolution is simply the theory of social alchemy.

Alchemy did not die out with the decline of alchemists in the eighteenth century. It simply gave way to a new form, to social and biological evolution. Evolution is alchemy brought up to date. It is the same, age-old dream, as ever appearing as true science, which offers to man the opportunity to be his own god.

Even Eliade, who is by no means an orthodox believer, states all the same: "We must not believe that the triumph of experimental science reduced to naught the dreams and ideals of the alchemists. On the contrary, the ideology of the new epoch, crystallized around the myth of infinite progress and boosted by the experimental sciences and the progress of industrialization which dominated and inspired the whole of the nineteenth century, takes up and carries forward—despite its radical secularization—the millenary dream of the alchemist." We can add that modern socialism and evolutionary thinking are even more rigorously forms of alchemy. Man dreams of remaking nature and conquering time. Man denies that God's law governs the universe, and that it governs absolutely. Instead, he sees all things as evolving out of chaos, and man seeks to govern that evolution by becoming himself *the principle of chaos.*

As a result, revolutionary man, the new principle of chaos, plunges the world into the abyss of revolution and chaos. Man creates planned chaos in every realm in the expectation of fertility. Not order but chaos rules in art. Art that moves in terms of law is regarded as dull, sterile, and academic. Planned chaos governs economics, and the economic law is denied. Education works to create rootlessness, which is allied to chaos, as a precondition of education and intellectualism. In every area, man creates revolution and chaos in the faith that a brave new world will thereby be born. The creative person is seen, not as the disciplined man, but as the undisciplined, chaotic person, a lawless creature whose every act is the ritual invocation of chaos. Bohemianism in art rests on this faith. The artist is an alchemist who can only invoke the basic fertility of the universe by means of chaos. By returning to chaos, he supposedly leaps ahead in time; he becomes the man of tomorrow, with more vigor and power because he is more lawless. In religion, we are told that conformity to God's infallible word is sterile and deadening. Man's religious freedom supposedly involves rebellion against God's ordered, final, and infallible truth. Man must turn from God's ordered world to the chaos and abyss of existentialism, and then, somehow, out of this will come forth true religion. The dark night of the soul as the chaos of unbeing is invoked as the way to the future.

In the nightmares of alchemy, in all its many forms, evolution and revolution, art and religion, wherever we meet it, there do we see the modern Babylonian captivity of man. Man is in Babylon, man is in a captivity of his own making. His own hands, his mind, science, religion, and politics have forged the chains of his new Babylonian captivity. Man is his own prisoner and his own tormentor. Man tortures himself with horrors of his own devising, and, denying God, calls out vainly to himself for help. Man has built a fresh Tower of Babel and is his own punishment and prison.

Alchemy, in all its modern forms, has been partially successful. It has created chaos successfully, but it has not brought a new order out of that chaos. It has successfully killed men, but it has not been able to make them alive. Instead of evolution, it has precipitated social devolution.

We cannot counteract alchemy except by means of a Biblical faith, one firmly grounded on creationism. In this is our hope of progress, our strength, and our security, and in Christ is our liberty. "They that trust in the LORD shall be as mount Zion, which cannot be removed, but abideth for ever" (Ps. 125:1). "The LORD reigneth; let the earth rejoice; let the multitude of isles be glad thereof" (Ps. 97:1). "For God is the King of all the earth: sing ye praises with understanding" (Ps. 47:7).

ELEVEN

LAW AND
ACADEMIC FREEDOM

One of the growing problems of our day is academic freedom. It is a subject which tends to breed intense feelings on both sides. The subject itself has ceased to be academic: it has become an issue of major social concern.

Let us examine, first of all, the argument of those who call themselves advocates of academic freedom. A good case in point is Emory University, a Methodist school, where Professor Thomas J. J. Altizer teaches. Altizer, whose position is basically Buddhist, is a leader of the "God-is-Dead Movement," and this is recognized by the College of Bishops, Southeastern Jurisdiction, of the Methodist Church. Of Altizer's arguments, the bishops said, "Such declarations are pure fantasy, unsupported by any responsible scientific knowledge, and contradicted by the long experience of man on the earth, and by the unnumbered millions who in the present know the Almighty as the living God." In passing, we can note that the bishops do not answer Altizer with the word of God, but rather with the experience of man. However, they do oppose Altizer. They do say, "We are amazed that a professor of the Bible and Religion in a church college should say…" such things. The bishops also make clear that Altizer does not speak for the Methodist Church, or for Emory University. "Professor Altizer speaks for himself only." The bishops reminded Altizer that "Freedom requires responsibility," but they made clear that "We are committed to the principle of academic freedom. A university presupposes freedom in the search for truth on the part of those associated with it." The bishops therefore urged full support of the university and expressed their pride in it.[1]

At the same time, the Development Office of Emory University issued a statement by William R. Cannon, Dean of the Chandler School of Theology, Emory University, "God is not Dead at Emory." Cannon, after making clear that Altizer teaches in Emory College, not in the School of Theology, affirms academic freedom. "When a person is brought to a faculty, he is given the opportunity to think freely and is encouraged, both in the laboratory and in the study, to engage in creative scholarship that will lead to new discoveries and open new frontiers of learning. To be sure, we run great risks in this; but the gains far outweigh the risks."

The Emory Board of Trustees Chairman, Henry L. Bowden, in a statement released to the press, November 30, 1965, affirmed the allegiance of Emory "to the principles of academic freedom as enumerated by the American Association of University Professors."

A similar issue cropped up in Berkeley, California, where the Berkeley Baptist Divinity School of the American Baptist Convention is located. Because of the liberalism of the faculty, many churches have withdrawn support. The president of the school saw this as denial of academic freedom, and, according to the Oakland *Tribune* for Sunday, December 4, 1966, "Dr. Arnott lashed out at those whose doctrinal beliefs do not allow for variance of opinion."

---

1. *Emory University and the Church*, The Southeaster Jurisdictional Council, The Methodist Church, Atlanta, Georgia, January 14, 1966.

Now certain presuppositions clearly appear from these various statements. *First,* academic freedom means that a teacher has the right to teach and write without any interference, even if his work is hostile to and subversive of the basic purpose of the school. *Second,* it is a merit when any school permits, tolerates, and encourages such teaching. *Third,* those who refuse to support teaching which is subversive of their faith are guilty of suppressing opinions and are regarded as hostile to liberty. *Fourth,* the basic function of any school is to encourage new ideas rather than propagate older ones.

Lest anyone assume that our description is unfair, let us note what the *Columbia Encyclopedia* has to say about "academic freedom":

> Academic freedom, right of scholars to pursue their research, to teach, and to publish without control or restraint from the institutions which employ them. This is a civil right that is enjoyed, at least in statute, by the citizens of democratic countries. In the case of scholars whose occupation is involved with that right, the concept of academic freedom generally includes the property right of tenure of office. An essential to the acceptance of the concept is the notion that truth is best discovered through the open investigation of all data. A less clearly developed corollary of academic freedom is the obligation of all those who enjoy it to pursue the line of open and thorough inquiry regardless of personal considerations. Historically, academic freedom developed in the period of the Enlightenment.

With this last sentence alone can we agree. This idea is a product of the Enlightenment and its rationalism, its belief in the god-like powers of the philosopher-kings. Like God, these thinkers assume they are objective, and like God, beyond any restraint by man. This is the essence of the modern doctrine of academic freedom: it insists implicitly that the scholars are the new gods of creation and are therefore beyond any control, any supervision, or any restraint. Our duty is to support them no matter what they do to us.

Let us examine this idea of academic freedom a little more closely; in actuality, it is a totalitarian doctrine which is hostile to real academic freedom. Academic freedom means, if taken literally, freedom of the academy, that is, freedom of the school. It means, or should mean, that anyone has the freedom to establish a school to propagate his ideas and to maintain that school without interference, as long as it does not violate the criminal and moral laws of society.

If the idea of academic freedom stated by *Columbia Encyclopedia*, the American Association of University Professors, and others were applied to religious freedom, and it is being applied, the result would be anarchy. It would mean that in every church every kind of religious idea would have equal rights. This would make it impossible to maintain the integrity of any church.

The same is true of colleges and universities. Let us assume that we, as a group of persons with a particular kind of religious faith, holding to a system of Christian theology, to a particular school of economics, a type of philosophy, and a very definite concept of education, established a college. The modern doctrine of academic freedom would *deny* us the right to have our kind of school; it would insist that we could have no standard of faith and character which we could require of all faculty members. The modern doctrine of academic freedom would rob us of the right of controlling our own school, because it would demand the total independence of all faculty members to be "without control or restraint." We would be obliged to support the school without any right of control, or else we would be called intolerant, fascistic, and many like names for withdrawing our support.

The practical result of this doctrine of academic freedom is the destruction of freedom. It denies us the right to establish schools to propagate, develop, and establish a particular faith and philosophy. This concept of academic freedom is a superb totalitarian doctrine, and an instrument for the destruction of any and every educational institution. No institution can be free to maintain its faith and philosophy when the total right of subversion is insisted on by the doctrine of so-called academic freedom. *All the rights, all the power, are placed in the hands of subversives by this idea of academic freedom.* The right to hold to a particular faith and philosophy, and to maintain a college in loyalty to that position, is specifically denied. The doctrine is called academic freedom, but it is actually *academic totalitarianism.*

That doctrine insists that freedom belongs only to that which is new and revolutionary, and it denies freedom to that which insists on loyalty to a given faith and philosophy. It is a viciously intolerant doctrine which, by a semantic trick, calls itself freedom when it is actually slavery.

No faith can exist if total right is given to its subversion, and the faith is denied the right to defend itself. The faith attacked by this so-called academic freedom doctrine is Christianity and its concept of absolute truth. The faith affirmed by this doctrine is the faith, as *Columbia Encyclopedia* indicated, of the Enlightenment, of humanism.

Now humanism has proved itself to be one of history's most savage and intolerant faiths. The history of humanism is one of terror, slavery, and persecution, but, in its rewriting of history, it accuses all others of these things. From the French Revolution to the present, this humanistic totalitarianism has been spreading its infection in all the world. The doctrine of academic freedom is one aspect of this totalitarian humanism. It is a doctrine advocating freedom for humanism only. It offers only destruction to all others, plus the requirement of continuing to support institutions which have betrayed the supporters.

Truly free education means that colleges must have the freedom to be themselves, to establish colleges based on a particular philosophy and to maintain that position against subversion. Atheistic colleges do not allow orthodox Christianity to be taught by their professors, but they call it a violation of academic freedom if a professor in a Christian college is not allowed to teach atheism. Call this by its right name; it is not a doctrine of freedom but of subversion and totalitarianism. True freedom involves the freedom for a college to be true to its faith. But the champions of this so-called academic freedom are not interested in freedom; they are for slavery, because they themselves are slaves, and their doctrine is one of academic enslavement. Beware of men who defend it.

TWELVE

Law and Magic

The modern mind tends to dismiss magic as something that belongs to the primitive state of mankind and with no relation of any vital sort to our present-day world. The reality of the matter is that magic is basic to the modern mentality, to our politics and science, and we cannot understand our present-day world without a knowledge of what magic is.

It is therefore important to know what magic is. Magic is the attempt by man to gain control over the world of man, nature, and the supernatural. In magic, man attempts to become god over all things and to assert his power and control over all reality. According to Kurt Koch:

> At the threshold of human history stands the command of God: Replenish the earth and subdue it (Gen. 1:28). The task and right of man was the peaceful conquest of the earth's powers in agreement with the will of God. In opposition to this command, Satan, the great master of confusion, made the arch-temptation: Ye shall be as gods, knowing good and evil (Gen. 3:5). The antithesis of the command of God is magic, hunger of knowledge and desire

for power in opposition to the will of God. With this, young mankind found itself at the crossroads.

The points are shifted: voluntary subordination under the will of God, or compulsion for knowledge and greed for power in rebellion against divine rules and barriers. Today these points are still shifted. Either we let ourselves be fit into the divine pattern of the way of salvation, or we carry on a rebellion and try to rule the powers of beings of creation in a monstrous rivalry with God. Therefore, magic is arch-rebellion from the beginning until today. It is the climax of man's revolt against God. All talk about harmless forces of nature and neutral application is an outrage in the face of this Biblical fact.[1]

It is thus obvious that magic is very much a part of our world today. Let us examine some areas in which magic appears.

Magic is very basic to modern science. The Biblical purpose of science is that man should seek knowledge in order that he might exercise dominion over the earth under God. Science in this sense is a necessary activity and sphere of knowledge for Christian cultures. But science today bypasses God and seeks to gain power without restraint and seeks knowledge as a tool of total power. Increasingly, science functions, not under the law of God, but as the new law of creation, as the new source of law and power. Instead of being governed by morality, science seeks to govern morality and to remake it in terms of its own standards. The purposes of science can be summed up as prediction, planning, and control. Science is thus a basic and essential part of the new politics, because their goals coincide; they are both clearly totalitarian. A scientific world is a controlled world, a world of experimentation, and valid experiments require a control of all factors. As a result, scientific society is a planned society, a society in which there is no liberty, because liberty is not possible in a situation of scientific planning. As a result, the more our culture is dominated by this

---

1. Kurt E. Koch, *Between Christ and Satan* (Grand Rapids: Kregel Publications, 1961), 77.

new science, apostate science, the more totalitarian it will become. Modern science not only rests on magic, it is a form of magic; it is the belief that all things can be potentially or ultimately controlled by man.

Our politics today is also governed by magic, by the faith that man can become his own god and remake the world to his heart's desire. The *techniques* of magic are no longer crude and primitive; they have been refined and developed into a science. But the *purposes* of magic remain unchanged and today govern both science and politics. The political orders of our world have separated themselves from Christianity, because they feel no need for God. They feel no need for God because they plan to become the new gods of creation. They plan to abolish sin and guilt, poverty, disease, and hunger, even death itself, and create a new paradise on earth. The new politics is a politics of total control, and it therefore hates God, because God represents a roadblock to power. God is the enemy who must be destroyed so that man can become his own god. The Fabian Socialist leader and teacher, G. D. H. Cole stated that an objective of socialism is the "abolition of God."[2] The logic of scientific socialism requires this goal. If man is to be the total agent of control, then God cannot be, and God must be abolished. The new politics is therefore the politics of anti-Christianity. It is the politics of magic. And magic has always been an enemy of Biblical faith. The Bible forbids magic, because magic is by its total nature in enmity to God. In a variety of passages, magic is strictly forbidden (e.g., Ex. 22:18; Lev. 19:26, 31; 20:6, 27; Deut. 18:10-11; Isa. 8:19; Micah 5:12; Mal. 3:5; Gal. 5:20; etc.). Its purpose, according to Scripture, is to divert people from God to man (Isa. 8:19).

Another important area where magic prevails today is in art. T. H. Robsjohn-Gibbings, in his study, *Mona Lisa's Mustache: A Dissection of Modern Art*, observed that "modern art is not modern at all. It is a revival of one of the oldest systems for

---

2. Rose L Martin, *Fabian Freeway: High Road to Socialism in the U.S.A, 1884-1966.* (Boston: Western Islands, 1966), 95.

getting power. It is a revival of magic."[3] The modern artists are totalitarians who despise man and liberty. As Robsjohn-Gibbings noted,

> According to the futurists, "Man has no more significance than a stone." We find Kandinsky, the leader of expressionism, writing haughtily of "the vulgar herd," and "the mob," we find the surrealists insisting on the "greatest possible obliteration of individuality," and Picasso, the leader of cubism, calling for "a dictatorship of one painter."
>
> To men such as these, art could be only a medium through which they would gain power over the fellow beings they consider so insignificant.[4]

The modern magical artist hates above all to be moral, law-abiding, and meaningful; he belongs in his imagination to an elite group whose purpose is to smash the present order and remake it totally in terms of their own elitist plans. According to one artist's manifesto, "The artist 'should be understood as a contemporary magician ... How are we to wield power; how are we to influence:' and not 'Are we scientists or poets?' is the question to be posed ... Seers, we are for the magic of life."[5] Modern art seeks to destroy God's meaning, to obliterate it from man's mind, so that man will no longer see God's order in things but will relearn all things as taught by magical art. Its purpose thus is total brainwashing.

Modern education is also dedicated to magic, to man's total control of all reality and man's remaking of all things in terms of human planning. State controlled schools have replaced religion with magic, and the goal of education today is the same as that of ancient magicians, the total control of all reality by man.

It is a serious error to treat magic as a relic of the past. The desire for magic is deeply imbedded in the heart of man. It is

---

3. T. H. Robsjohn-Gibbings, *Mona Lisa's Mustache: A Dissection of Modern Art* (n.p.: Knopf, 1947), 13.
4. Ibid., 15.
5. Cited from T. H. Robsjohn-Gibbings, *View*, 175.

basic to his original sin. Satan's temptation was "Ye shall be as gods, knowing [that is, determining, or establishing for yourself] good and evil" (Gen. 3:5). Man, by his own will can become god; he is told by Satan that he can not only become his own god and remake all things according to his will but that his will is creative and determinative. What man wishes, that man can do. Every vagrant dream of man's sinful and proud heart magic tells him is a possibility. And now modern science and the new politics, scientific socialism, tell man that they are about to make real this magical hope. The appeal of scientific socialism is the appeal of magic. It is the belief that man's imagination rather than Almighty God is the ultimate governing and creating force in the universe.

Every belief in magic is therefore firmly set on a collision course; collision with God's purpose and judgment is inescapable. Because the science and politics of magic openly declare war against God and His government, they invite that collision, and they invite it in the confidence that they shall kill God and abolish Him. In their pride, they cannot tolerate the thought that there is a God over them. Friedrich Nietzsche, in *Thus Spoke Zarathustra* wrote: "But that I may reveal my heart entirely unto you, my friends: *if* there were Gods, how could I endure it to be no God! *Therefore* there are no Gods."[6] In other words, Nietzsche's main objection to God was that he himself was not God; therefore, he declared there can be no God if I cannot be one. Having "abolished" God, Nietzsche proceeded to declare himself a god and also the creator of a new world, for "what would there be to create if there were—Gods!"[7] This is the mind and world of pure magic, and its conclusion, as in Nietzsche's life, is madness and some form of self-destruction.

We face, then, a conflict between two worlds of law, the law of God, versus the law of magic, of the new politics, science, and education, of humanism in its essence. Of the conclusion there can be no doubt. The Psalmist said of Christ the King,

---

6. Friedrich Nietzsche, *Thus Spoke Zarathustra*, Part II, xxiv.
7. Ibid.

"Thou shalt break them with a rod of iron; thou shalt dash them in pieces like a potter's vessel. Be wise now therefore, O ye kings: be instructed, ye judges of the earth ... Blessed are all they that put their trust in him" (Ps. 2:9, 12).

THIRTEEN

LAW AND GOVERNMENT

It is difficult nowadays to discuss government because the word *government* has radically changed its meaning. In my book, *This Independent Republic*, I pointed out that originally the word government was never applied in this country to the state. The world government meant, *first* of all, the self-government of the Christian man, the basic government in all history. *Second*, and very closely and almost inseparably linked with this, government meant the family. Every family is a government; it is man's first church and first school, and also his first state. The government of the family by God's appointed head, the man, is basic to society. *Third*, the church is a government, with laws and discipline. *Fourth*, the school is an important government in the life of a child. *Fifth*, business or vocations are an important area of government. Our work clearly governs us and we govern our work. *Sixth*, private associations, friendships, organizations, and the like act as a government over us, in that we submit to these social standards and we govern others by our social expectations. *Seventh*, the state is a form of government, and, originally, it was always called *civil* government in distinction from all these other forms of government.

But, tragically, today when we say *government*, we mean the state, the federal government, or some other form of civil government. And, more tragically, civil government today claims to be *the* government over man, not one government among many, but the one over-all government. Civil government claims jurisdiction over our private associations, our work or business, our schools and churches, our families, and over ourselves. The word government no longer means self-government primarily and essentially, it means the state.

But, originally, in our Christian American heritage, government did not mean the state. Some object that, while this was true in the colonial period, the picture changed after the War of Independence. The answer to that is to examine a textbook used in public high schools and in normal schools prior to World War I, Alex L. Peterman's *Elements of Civil Government*. Peterman was principal and professor of civil government in the Normal School of the Kentucky State College and also a member of the Kentucky State Senate. Notice also that Peterman's title speaks of *civil* government.

The preface stated, "This textbook begins 'at home.' The starting point is the family, the first form of government with which the child comes in contact."[1] According to Peterman, "The family ... is a form of government, established for the good of the children themselves, and the first government that each of us must obey."[2] The first chapter of Peterman's textbook was devoted to "The Family," its purpose, members, rights, duties, officers, and responsibilities. It is interesting to see that Peterman wrote that "The office of a parent is a holy office, and requires wisdom for the proper discharge of its duties."[3] Peterman's perspective on civil government was clearly one of a division of powers and federalism. He defined

---

1. Alex L. Peterman, *Elements of Civil Government* (New York: American Book Company, 1891, 1903), 5.
2. Ibid., 18.
3. Ibid., 19.

five areas of civil government: "the township or civil district, the village or the city, the county, the State, and the Untied States."[4] But, most important, as recently as World War I, civil government was a minor area of government in American life; now, civil government claims to be *the* overall government in man's life. This claim is the essence of totalitarianism. From the self-government of the Christian man as the essence of government we have gone to the idea of the state as the totalitarian ruler over man.

When we raise the question, "How did this happen?" two answers are immediately available. *First*, we can say that we have been subverted by revolutionary and totalitarian groups, and, *second*, we can say that our own spiritual delinquency has led us into this sorry condition. Clearly, there is truth in the first answer. We have been the target of subversive activity in every area, and highly trained and skilled subversive agents have been at work in our midst for many years. However, there has never been a period in American history when subversives have not been active, nor has there ever been a civilization in all history without a challenge from hostile forces. The important fact to remember is that we will always be challenged by some kind of subversion; the real question is this: Do we have the spiritual health to resist the challenge? If we are spiritually and morally delinquent, we are easily subverted. In contrast to the millions of Americans, the subversive forces are numerically small, even if we estimate them in the millions. Our problem is not primarily what others are trying to do to us but what we have done to ourselves. The subversives are real and they are deadly, but they are helpless against a spiritually strong people.

Today, most Americans have lost their faith in Christ as Savior, and they expect civil government to be their savior. They have no desire for the responsibilities of self-government, and so they say to politicians, "Do thou rule over us." Instead of Jesus Christ as their good shepherd, they elect politicians to be

---

4. Ibid., 18.

their shepherds on a program of socialistic security for all. Is it any wonder that we are subverted?

To have free civil government it is necessary first of all to have free men whose greatest desire is responsible self-government under God. Not many men are interested in this. A professor, who had left teaching soon after World War II, lectured to a group of students at a major Western university a few years ago on the decline of liberty. To his shock, one of the first questions asked by a student was simply this: "What's so wonderful about liberty? What makes you think it is necessary for man?" For the students, security was a necessary social objective; liberty was not. Some years ago, Lin Yutang reported that, before he came to the United States, he thought of America in terms of Patrick Henry's words, "Give me liberty or give me death." When he came here, he found that the modern American creed seems to be "Give me security or give me death." It is because we are refusing to govern ourselves under God and by God's grace and word that we are being governed by the state. As William Penn and Benjamin Franklin long ago noted, men will either be governed by God, or they will be governed by tyrants. Americans are being subverted, and they have themselves to blame most of all for it.

Our breakdown is secondarily political; it is primarily spiritual. Our subversion is secondarily political; it is primarily spiritual.

The *basic* government of the universe and of man is the government of God. Every person, family, institution, vocation, school, church, or state which is in rebellion against God's government or bypasses His word and law is thereby in rebellion against its own health, against its own life. According to St. Paul, the law of God was ordained to life, or, as the Berkeley version translated it, the law "aimed to give life" (Rom. 7:10), but man's sin has made it a death sentence. Jesus Christ, speaking as Wisdom, said long ago, "He that sinneth against me wrongeth his own soul: all they that hate me love death" (Prov. 8:36).

Wherever any government departs from God and His law it departs from health and ultimately from life. The government of God is basic to self-government, to the family, church, school, society, vocations, and to the state. It would be ridiculous for man to plan a life and a future in which air is abolished, because, obviously, man needs the air to breathe, to survive, to live; his life depends on it. Even more fundamentally, man's life depends on the government of God; it is the essential for life in every sphere of existence.

Self-government presupposes freedom, and there can be no true freedom for man apart from Jesus Christ. Christ is our principle of liberty, the source and power of man's deliverance from the slavery of sin and the penalty of death. Jesus declared, "I am the way, the truth, and the life (John 14:6). "[Y]e shall know the truth, and the truth shall make you free" (John 8:32). "If the Son therefore shall make you free, ye shall be free indeed" (John 8:36). This is the foundation of liberty and of true self-government. Apart from this foundation, Jesus Christ, our destiny is tyranny and slavery. In Jesus Christ alone is our liberty assured and true government possible.

FOURTEEN

LAW & PROPERTY

Before there can be any possibility of a just social order, there must be a true understanding of property and its meaning. Property rights are seriously challenged in our day by socialism, and they are attacked as a roadblock to human rights. Socialists are not against property as such; they are hostile to private property, and they transfer all or most property rights to the state.

Biblical law speaks very clearly about property. *First* of all, it declares that all property, the earth itself and all creation, belongs to God. God declared to Israel that "all the earth is mine" (Ex. 19:5). "I am God ... every beast of the forest is mine, and the cattle upon a thousand hills ... the wild beasts of the forest is mine ... the world is mine, and the fullness thereof" (Ps. 50:7, 10–12). The New Testament restates this principle: "the earth is the Lord's and the fullness thereof" (1 Cor. 10:26, 28); "all things are of God" (2 Cor. 5:18). God is thus the absolute Lord over all property, and therefore His law governs all property.

Second, God established man in the possession of property under God as a basic aspect of the life of the family and as an essential of the economy of the family. Two of the Ten Commandments govern property: "Thou shalt not steal," and "Thou shalt not covet thy neighbour's house ... nor anything that is thy neighbour's" (Ex. 20:15, 17).

Third, God made property man's basic earthly security, and a man's home is his castle in God's law. The Bible did not have provision for any property tax; indeed, it saw it only as a form of tyranny and confiscation (1 Sam. 8:7-18). The only tax God required or permitted on property was the tithe to God. The property tax is thus properly God's tax, and a voluntary tax, depending on man's faith and obedience. Originally, none of the American states permitted a property tax, and all were hostile to it. On November 8, 1966, Nebraska voters abolished state property taxes and rejected also a state income tax.[1] In Biblical law, laws of inheritance were not state laws but family laws, and their purpose was twofold—to protect the family, and to protect the property. Because the state could not tax property, a man was secure in his land, home, and possessions in good times and bad.

Fourth, the Biblical law protected the family and property as an essential unit. Rand has noted,

> The law of the Lord abounds with safeguards placed around the family, protecting the family, keeping it pure from pollution and punishing those who violate the sanctity of the home. No property rights were more rigidly guarded and protected than the rights of man and wife, with the death penalty pronounced upon adulterers.[2]

The basic principle is this: the law protects the family and its property from interference by the state, or by an adulterous person. The family depends on property for its material independence, and property depends on the family for its

---

1. *The Wall Street Journal,* Tuesday, November 29, 1966, "What's News," 1.

2. Howard B. Rand, *Digest of the Divine Law* (Merrimac, MA: Destiny Publishers, [1943] 1959), 107.

meaning and protection. This relationship, although distorted and misrepresented, has been seen by socialists as witness Friedrich Engels' study, *The Origin of the Family, Private Property, and the State* (1891). For such men, the abolition of private property requires also the abolition of the family; it is impossible to eliminate the one successfully without eliminating the other.

The Bible linked property and family so closely together that a man could not dispose of his property and live off the proceeds and thereby harm his children's inheritance (Lev. 25:23). The laws protecting property are very many, and the Bible gives them central attention.[3] Property was thus protected for the family from the state by being immune from taxation; property was protected for the family from other persons by strict laws against adultery, which is destructive of the family. Property was further protected for the family from the family itself; the father had no right to spend it on himself or to alienate it from the family.

Fifth, basic to the Biblical law of liberty for man is property. When a man is secure in the possession of his property, he has an area of liberty and dominion that is beyond the reach of other men. If no man and no state can reach in to tax or to confiscate this property, man can enjoy true liberty and great security, whether he be prosperous or poor. Every attack on private property is, therefore, an attack on man's liberty. Man's freedom and security in the possession of his property is not only basic to man's independence, but it is also basic to his power. A man has power if he can act independently of other men and the state, if he can make his stand in the confidence of liberty. Every attack on private property therefore is also an attack on the powers of free men as well as their liberty.

It follows therefore that a transfer of property from man to the state is a transfer of liberty and power from the people to the state. The necessary way for any state to become powerful

---

3. Roger Sherman Galer, *Old Testament Law for Bible Students* (New York: Macmillan, 1922), 77–113.

and totalitarian is to restrict and suddenly or gradually confiscate and abolish private property. No new set of legislators can stop or stem any state's march towards total power if they leave untouched the state's power over property, real property, personal property, and monetary property. No groups of "reform" politicians have kept their promises unless they set property free from statist control and intervention.

One reason for the decline of private property in recent years has been the doctrine of evolution. Evolution sees no absolute law of God governing private property. Instead, it sees property as a part of man's evolution out of the primal horde into modern culture. Most evolutionists see property as a late and ugly development; others see it as a good one. In either case, property has no ultimate and fundamental moral sanction behind it; it is simply a product of evolutionary development and is therefore subject to change.

Marxism depends heavily on this evolutionary foundation. For Marxism, the state is man's organization and power for the maintenance of private property; when the family and private property are abolished, the state will disappear also, and communism will replace it. Private property was and is defined as theft by Marxism. Marxism sees it as a social necessity to destroy the thieves, the propertied classes, and to supplant them with communism. In attacking property, Marxism attacks with it not only the family but God as well. It sees, and correctly so, God, the family, and property as inseparably linked by nature and by law.

Every defense of property therefore is ineffective and paralyzed if it simply seeks to defend private property without at the same time defending the family and Christianity. This is the fallacy of the libertarians who seek to defend private property in isolation from Christian faith and the family. Too often, by this limited approach, they not only begin with two strikes on them but also more than partially in the enemy's camp.

It follows therefore, as a *sixth* point, that every attack on private property is also an attack on God, because the one real foundation for private property is the law of God. The Marxists have made little attempt to conceal their war against God and their war against the family and its property. For them, all three must go. Christianity, by establishing God's absolute lordship over the earth and by grounding private property in the word of God, alone gives to private property any real security. The roots of private property grow weak when Biblical faith grows weak.

Seventh, private property and moral order are closely linked together. When men are governed by God, they are more provident, more inclined to be debt-free, more responsible in their management of their families and affairs, and much more prone to own, cherish and husband property wisely. A high incidence of debt-free property indicates a high degree of godly living which is both provident and free of covetousness, for it is covetousness that breeds debt-living. The basic principle of Scripture is very clear-cut: "Owe no man anything, but to love one another" (Rom. 13:8). We do not truly own property unless it is debt-free. Debt is in essence a form of slavery, and the basic function of private property is to establish us in material liberty. A man who covets property of various kinds but cannot live debt-free is not seeking property on godly terms but on covetous terms. In Colossians 3:5, St. Paul defines evil covetousness as idolatry, and he declares that it is a sin that we must mortify or destroy in ourselves. Such covetousness seeks to exalt the man and to increase his possessions, but because it grounds itself on sin rather than God's law, it is destructive of both man and property. Those who move in terms of God's word become the blessed meek, the tamed of God, of whom the Psalmist says, "The meek shall inherit the earth; and shall delight themselves in the abundance of peace" (Ps. 37:11).

FIFTEEN

THE FAMILY
AND PROPERTY

All kinds of reasons are assigned for the decline of the family, both spiritual and material, and we are repeatedly told of the social consequences of the breakdown of family life. However, in all these reports on the family, one important cause is commonly left out, a cause which is at one and the same time both material and spiritual. This cause for the breakdown of the family is the attack on and the decline of the freedom of private property.

Private ownership of property was ordained by God and firmly grounded in His law. Four of the Ten Commandments deal with family and property: "Honour thy father and thy mother"; "Thou shalt not commit adultery"; "Thou shalt not steal"; and "Thou shalt not covet thy neighbor's house, thou shalt not covet they neighbor's wife, nor his manservant, nor his maidservant, nor his ox, nor his ass, nor any thing that is thy neighbor's" (Ex. 20:12, 14-15, 17). According to the Bible, the family is more than a spiritual unity; it is a material unity, firmly grounded in property and economic realities. Similarly, private property is not merely a neutral material thing for the

Bible; it is essentially linked to God's spiritual realities, His law, and the family. The property and family are everywhere closely linked together by the Bible. Every attack therefore on private property is an attack on the family, and every attack on the family is also an attack on private property. This unity of the family and property has been recognized by Marxism, and as a result both are marked for destruction in Communist countries.

In 1847, in the *Communist Manifesto*, Karl Marx wrote, "the theory of the Communists may be summed up in a single sentence: Abolition of private property." Any kind of property, he noted, is *power*, and he denied the right of power to the person or family; it had to be "social power." The family, he said, is based on capital, private gain, private property, and he added that the family "will vanish with the vanishing of capital." To achieve the goal of communization, Marx favored the state control of all education, and he criticized what he called "The bourgeois clap-trap about the family and education, about the hallowed correlation of parent and child." Thus, replacing Christian schools with state-controlled and state-supported schools was for Marx a necessary step towards destroying the family and private property.

The abolition of what Marx called "bourgeois marriage" is another step. Other steps cited by Marx included abolition of property in land, abolition of all right of inheritance, the income tax, the requirement that women and children must work, and so on.

As against God's Ten Commandments, Marx, very self-consciously, stated his new law in ten points or laws:

1. Abolition of private property in land and the application of all rents of land to public purposes.

2. A heavy progressive or graduated income tax.

3. Abolition of all rights of inheritance.

4. Confiscation of the property of all emigrants and rebels.

5. Centralization of credit in the hands of the state, by means of a national bank with state capital and an exclusive monopoly.

6. Centralization of the means of communication and transportation in the hands of the state.

7. Extension of factories and instruments of production owned by the state; the bringing into cultivation of waste lands, and the improvement of the soil generally in accordance with a common plan.

8. Equal liability of all to labor. Establishment of industrial armies, especially for agriculture.

9. Combination of agriculture with manufacturing industries; gradual abolition of the distinction between town and country by a more equable distribution of the population over the country.

10. Free education for all children in government schools. Abolition of children's factory labor in its present form. Combination of education with industrial production, etc., etc.

Except for Marx's program for a new form of child labor, every one of these points is in operation in part or in whole in our country today, and the *Communist Manifesto* is a better expression of our social and political goals and direction than anything said by either political party. We are very clearly drifting into communism.

Now Marx was very wise in his analysis, and Marx saw clearly the implications of Biblical economy and of the Ten Commandments: *property is power, social and personal power. Whoever controls property has liberty, and whoever surrenders power over property surrenders liberty.* The question then is simply this: who shall be free, the family or the state? God's law provides for the freedom of the family by undergirding private ownership of property. The American tradition has been Biblical. The purpose of the Constitution of 1787 was to bind the federal government with the chains of the Constitution so that the people might be free. If civil government is given power over property, then that government becomes free from the control of its citizenry and controls them instead. Today, the state has extensive controls over property and taxes it; there is an inheritance tax and an income tax. There is state controlled education, and centralization of credit in the hands of the state. There is control over capital, labor, and farming. Is it any wonder the family is breaking down and the federal government growing in power. The God-given economic foundation of the family is being destroyed, because God's law is despised. There is no combating the Marxist system without a return to Biblical faith.

Marx was right: *property is power*, and God places this power in the family's hands. The authority of the family requires property. In Communist countries, it is a routine and normal thing for children to spy on their parents and report their remarks and activities to the state. Power and authority belong to the state, and therefore the allegiance of children is to the state. Their future rests with the state, and therefore it is the state they obey and the state whom they seek to please.

Biblical law places power and authority into the hands of the parents, especially the father, and, as long as the family has liberty, liberty based on the power of property, the parents have authority. The primary purpose of the inheritance tax has been to destroy this parental power; the total financial gain to the state by means of inheritance taxes is small. Similarly, transfer of power over education, income, and property from the family to the state has undercut parental power and authority.

Because the modern state controls the education, income, property, and labor of *all* its citizens, it thus controls the totality of powers within the country. The result is totalitarianism. Every country that weakens the independence and liberty of the family and property moves steadily into totalitarianism. It makes no difference in which country this occurs, and what laws the state passes as a restraint on itself. *Property is power, and when the state grows in its controls over property, it grows in the same degree towards totalitarian power.* No political program can stop this growth unless it restores to the family its control over property, income, and education. As long as the state retains the control, it will retain the power and the authority, and it is naïve and absurd to expect anything but tyranny.

The future of the family is thus at stake in the future of the private ownership of property. And both rest alike on respect for the sovereign law of God. It is significant that the Ten Commandments have four which protect the family and property and not one which protects the state. Now elsewhere Scripture speaks about respect for civil rulers, and it calls for respect and obedience where obedience is due. But the state is not given a place by name in the Ten Commandments, and, for that matter, neither is the church, although worship is governed by the first four commandments. The only institution which directly appears in the Ten Commandments is the family, and to it clearly is given authority over property by the whole of the law.

Moreover, the Biblical family is placed under God, and therefore it is denied the totalitarian power that some Oriental systems, with ancestor worship, give to the family to its own detriment. The Biblical family, with its liberty in property, is the foundation of Western liberty. To defend the family, therefore, without a defense of its God-given economic foundation is both wrong and futile, and to defend property without securing its religious foundations is to defend it ignorantly and vainly. "Except the LORD build the house, they labour in vain that build it" (Ps. 127:1).

SIXTEEN

THE FAMILY
AND INHERITANCE

Property is power, and the control of property is therefore the key to power. Basic to all control of property is the control of inheritance. According to the *Columbia Encyclopedia*, inheritance in law is the "right to acquire *property* on the death of the owner... In Anglo-American law inheritance is by the grace of the state, which may exercise any degree of control over the property of the decedent (i.e., the owner who dies), including the total escheat (i.e., government acquisition of title)." "By the grace of the state"! And how much grace does a state have? Since when has the state been the source of grace?

When the state enters into the question of inheritance, property gradually is transferred from the family to the state. The inheritance tax is simply a first step in that program of confiscation. For the family to maintain itself, the family must control inheritance, and the Biblical laws of inheritance are entirely family laws. The Bible kept property immune from taxation and from anything but family control of inheritance.

Inheritance, according to the Bible, was a sign of faith, character, and godliness on the part of a man. The Bible declares, "A good man leaveth an inheritance to his children's children" (Prov. 13:22). And, as H. B. Clark, a law editor, stated in his study of *Biblical Law,* "There is nothing in Jewish law to warrant the belief that the King or the State has any right to inherit property upon the death of the owner without proper heirs." The control of property and inheritance is entirely within the jurisdiction of the family in Biblical law.

What was the consequence of the Biblical law of inheritance? It meant simply that power was concentrated into the hands of the family. This meant that the authority of the family over its children was a very real one, and an undiminished power. The discipline of parents over their children was unquestioned, because authority and economic power rested in the family. The Bible is a realistic book. God knows that man respects authority which has power behind it. When an order is given, that order is futile unless it can be supported by the power to enforce it. If power is transferred from the family to the state, then the ability to give orders and to maintain order is transferred from the family to the state. Educational philosophers begin to speak of "the children of the state," because parental authority has been transferred to the state.

According to Carle C. Zimmerman and Lucius F. Cervantes, in their study, *Marriage and Family,* Western society has had a family organization since Christianity became the faith of the West. A man's life, from birth to death, is guided, affected, and colored by family relations. The basic unit of the social order is the family. The family is the socially stable unit where the family has liberty and property.

As a result, the totalitarians hate the family and declare it to be the enemy of social change. Totalitarianism hates the family because it is the basic thesis of all totalitarians that man's first loyalty must be to the state, whereas the Christian family's first allegiance is to the triune God. The totalitarian therefore seeks to abolish the family. Lenin said, "No nation can be free when half the population is enslaved in the kitchen." As a result, the Communist state abolished the family as a legal entity until 1936, and the family since then has merely been a legal breeding ground for the state. The Soviet Union, two years after the Revolution, announced, "The family has ceased to be a necessity, both for its members and for the State." Women were "freed" from the kitchen only to become the unskilled labor force of the Soviet Union. According to Zimmerman and Cervantes, among the means taken by the Soviet Union "to abolish the family" were the following:

> [T]he forbidding of parents to give religious instruction to their children, the encouraging of children to denounce their parents, the abolishing of inheritance, the equalization of the "non-registered marriage" with the registered one, the promulgation of three forms of common ménage contract: for an indefinite period, for a definite period, for a single occasion. This latter legal expedient was a propaganda piece aimed to demolish the difference between prostitution, promiscuity, and monogamy. The legalization of bigamy and the abolishing of the legal differences between legitimacy and illegitimacy were other minor steps with the same purport of the destruction of the family.

"Free love in a free state" became the ideal. Family life was declared to be "especially harmful to collective life."[1]

In the United States, the attack on the family is being steadily mounted. The state increasingly claims jurisdiction over the family, its children, income, and property. The state assumes that it knows what is best for children, and it claims the right to interfere for the children's welfare. As a result, the family is progressively weakened in order to strengthen the power of the state. The authority of parents is legally weakened and children are given legal rights to undercut their parents. According to Zimmerman and Cervantes, the reality today in our courts is a very startling one. They report:

> Thus in New York, Chicago, and Boston, children are now allowed to sue second spouses of a parent some years later

---

1. Carle C. Zimmerman and Lucius F. Cervantes, *Marriage and the Family* (Chicago: Regnery, 1956), 525.

for "alienation" of love and affection of the parent. In New York and Chicago, the children have won these cases, but they are still pending in Boston. Thus, also, we have the New York case where a divorced mother—custodian of children—was imprisoned for neglect some years after the divorce. The husband was safe because he was not given custody, although the earlier "discoloration" theory would have blamed him also.[2]

Such powers, when given to the child, are not for the child's welfare. They are destructive of the family and of the child, and the more the state legislates over the family, supposedly for its welfare, the more it destroys the family.

No institution can long exist if it is not free. The more controlled an institution becomes, the less life it has. Its life and functions are transferred to the controlling agent, or they simply cease to be. How long would a club last, if its every act were controlled by the state? The life and authority of the family depends on the liberty of the family, and the economic expression of the family's independence is the right to private ownership of property and the right of inheritance.

Now where the family controls inheritance, it also controls marriage. This Friedrich Engels noted in his study of *The Origin of the Family, Private Property, and the State.* But the Bible long ago plainly recorded it. When Jacob became the heir, his father Isaac "blessed him and charged him, and said unto him, Thou shalt not take a wife of the daughters of Canaan" (Gen. 28:1). In other words, the father had the power to require a godly marriage; because Isaac was leaving a sizable inheritance, he had a stake in the future, and because he had a stake in that future, he had a right to control it by requiring a godly marriage. This was a legitimate and godly power. The Bible as a result gives a great deal of space to laws of inheritance. Roger Sherman Galer, in his classification of Biblical law, takes more than seven pages merely to list these laws.[3]

---

2. Ibid., 598
3. Roger Sherman Galer, *Old Testament Law for Bible Students* (New York: Macmillan, 1922), 85-101.

Where the father possesses private property and provides for his children's care and future, and controls their inheritance, it is the authority of the father which governs the family. Where the state assumes the responsibility for the welfare and education of the children, and assures them of future social security, it is the authority of the state which governs the children. Power over private property is authority. Where the state controls property, income, and inheritance, power has been transferred to the state. Honor and authority go hand in hand, and, where parents have authority, they are more readily honored. The Biblical law declares, "Honour thy father and thy mother: that thy days may be long upon the land which the LORD thy God giveth thee" (Ex. 20:12). It is because God gave this law that He gave also the laws concerning private ownership of property and the right of inheritance. The two go hand in hand. God forbids adultery, because He has ordained and established the family as the basic and central social unit of mankind. God therefore commands private ownership of property and private control of inheritance in order that the family may be maintained in its honor and authority. We do not honor the family or parents if we strip them of their powers.

In fact, we are now being told that the family is obsolete. One prominent and influential churchman has said that the family is, like the tribe, a relic of the past. The tribe served its purpose and is now gone; the family, a great institution for its time, has also seen its day, and it must make way for a new structuring of society.

The death of the family is therefore planned, and, on every continent, the executioners are at work. Together with the death of the family, the "death" of God is also proclaimed, and we are assured that the new age has no need for God or the family. The menace and intensity of dedication of these hostile forces cannot be underestimated. They are an active, powerful, and highly organized force in modern society.

But, even more, we dare not underestimate the power of the triune God, Who rules the nations and fulfils His holy purpose despite all the vain conspiracies and wild imaginations of men. But none can share in God's victory unless they stand forth clearly in terms of Him and His holy cause, unless they separate themselves unto Him. Jesus Christ said, "He that is not with me, is against me: and he that gathereth not with me, scattereth abroad" (Matt. 12:30). And you, where do you stand?

SEVENTEEN

THE FUNCTIONS
OF THE FAMILY

H istorically and Biblically, the family is the central institution in law and in society. Although we do not think of the family normally as a lawmaking body, the family is nonetheless the basic lawmaking body in all history. Every point of power and authority is also a point of law, and, historically, family law has been the basic law of mankind. In any society or institution, there are basic rules of conduct, and these rules of conduct constitute its law structure. The family is man's basic lawmaking body because of a variety of reasons, but certainly one of the first of these is the fact that it is the first place man, as a child, encounters law, rules of conduct, and his idea of law is shaped and defined to a great degree by the family. Life is seen through a law structure which the family gives to the child, and this law structure defines life for the child. But this is not all. The child's attitude towards every other institution and its laws is largely shaped by the family. How the child approaches and reacts to church, school, state, and society depends greatly on his source of law, parental authority. He can face other lawmaking bodies rebelliously, or he can face them obediently. His attitude can be constructive, destructive, or indifferent, depending on his family background to a large degree. Every parent daily is a lawmaking person, a focal point of law enforcement, and the delinquency of parents in this respect is their delinquency before God, their Lord and sovereign.

It is obvious, of course, that procreation, birth, is a function of the family, and, in a healthy, Biblically oriented and governed family system, this function is preceded by an important fact that conditions birth. The parents marry because there is a bond of faith and love between them, a resolution to maintain for life a covenant under God. As a result, a heredity of faith and a unity in terms of it are established as a prior condition of birth, so that a child born into such a family has an inheritance which cannot be duplicated. The Biblical family cannot be rivaled by man's science or imagination as the institution for the procreation and rearing of children.

Moreover, the family is man's first and basic school. Parents have very extensively educated their children before the child ever sets foot inside a school. Moreover, every mother regularly performs the most difficult of all educational tasks, one which no school performs. The mother takes a small child, incapable of speaking or understanding a word in any language, and, in a very short time, teaches it the mother tongue. This is a difficult and painstaking task, but it comes simply and naturally in the family as an expression of the mother's love and the child's response to that love. At every stage of the child's life, the educational function of the home is the basic educational power in the life of the child. For education to cease to be parent-controlled and become state-controlled is deadly to both education and the child.

The family is also the first government in the life of the child, with the father as the God-ordained head of the household and his government under God as the child's basic government. The children are not the only ones who are governed by the family; the parents are also. The mother is governed in her activities by the requirements of her husband and children. The father is governed by the necessities of providing for his family, protecting them, and giving them the example and leadership they need. Where the family is not self-supporting, there is neither power nor authority in the person of the father. Welfare families, from the days of the Roman Empire to the present, have been notorious for the undisciplined, immoral, and delinquent characters, and welfare families have always been marked by a general lack of masculine authority. A man who will not provide for his family, accumulate respect, and cherish private property, will have neither the authority nor the ability to govern with wisdom and honor. Lacking self-government, he cannot govern others. Welfare destroys family life and creates more evils than it tries to solve.

Another basic function of the family is motivation and guidance. The child is provided with the best kind of guidance, because the family is most interested in him, and the child is, in the Christian family, given the highest kind of motivation for his own future and present development.

The family also has a major economic function. The father provides for his family, not for strangers. Welfare agencies maintained by state and federal agencies have provided some kind of economic existence for as many as fifteen and more millions at one time. But, daily, far more than a hundred million persons are supported by the family system. Under statist welfare, there is disintegration of the individual and of the family and extensive demoralization. Under the family system, untold millions are supported ably and well, with the best of social consequences. Under welfare, education declines; there is less interest in the discipline and results of learning, and less ability to progress as a result. Under the family system, children are not only intellectually motivated for the best educational results, but they are economically financed through grade and high school, college, and sometimes graduate school, so that the most ambitious educational enterprise of history is economically dependent on the family system. In terms of sheer economic efficiency, nothing in all of history has ever equaled the family. By comparison, statist welfare and

Communist takeovers of the family's economic functions are pathetic and tragic failures. Socially, this magnificent economic institution, the family, has no equal in its contribution to social stability and order. To reduce the reason for marriage and the family to love is to deny the vast and varying social functions of the family. But, in the Biblical perspective, the family and marriage are governed, not by love as the only sufficient reason, or the social consequences, but by the covenant with God and the Word of God.

The family as an economic unit has an excellent division of labor plan, whereby certain duties are required of the father, others of the mother, and still others of the children. There are mutual rights and duties, all of which are discharged with a greater degree of success and efficiency, despite all the problems, than in any other institution. The family, moreover, can withstand and survive more shock than any other institution—economic disasters, personal disagreements, social catastrophes, and the like.

The family has also a valuable policing and protective function. The members of a family police one another; they work to keep their members in line and out of trouble. The members of a family not only police and punish one another, but they also protect one another, and theirs is a cradle-to-grave protective function. When civil governments talk about cradle-to-grave security, they are simply imitating the family and offering the state as a substitute for the family. Throughout history and today, the family has provided cradle-to-grave security for the overwhelming majority of all men and has done a most satisfactory job of it. The state has botched up its every attempt to replace the family. Today, the state has worked to limit the authority, power, and ability of the family and then has turned to blame the family for conditions the state has created.

The state has extensively interfered in the family's functions, and it has claimed vast areas that properly belong to the family. Does this mean that the family has been weakened? Does the future portend a decline in the importance of the family? On the contrary, the more the state has interfered, the more it has thereby underscored man's need for the family. The incompetence of the state as family has made more obvious the competence of the family as a family. The prevalence of sickness does not make health obsolete, but only all the more urgently needed and desired. Historically, every period of statism is followed by an era of an intensely family-oriented society as men turn from sickness to health.

We are today in an era of burgeoning statism. On every side, the family is under attack, and the state is assuming progressively more and more of the family's functions, and progressively finding itself more and more prone to social disintegration and demoralization. More than ever before, the Biblical faith and law concerning the family, its functions, property, and *faith*, must be stressed and taught. The future does not belong to disease; it belongs to health. Because this is God's world, it is God's order which shall prevail. "Except the LORD build the house, they labour in vain that build it" (Ps. 127:1).

EIGHTEEN

THE FOUNDATIONS
OF THE FAMILY

The foundation of family and marriage in contemporary thinking is romantic love. The motivation which brings two people together to unite in marriage is very commonly romantic love and too often little else.

Romantic love as the motive of marriage is not a new force in history. It has a long history behind it. In Roman history, even more plainly, sexual love was held to be, by the third century of the Christian era, the best reason for marriage. In terms of this idea of marriage, it was expected that the man rival the gods as a great lover, while the woman was expected to out-Venus Venus. Technique in marriage was held to be everything, and anyone not interested in sexual sophistication was despised as an amateur. Instead of increasing marital happiness, this Roman emphasis on sexual love only intensified marital disharmony and increased the breakdown of marriage and family.

Simultaneously with this Roman development of sexual love as the ground of marriage, there was a growing contempt for and an attack on the institution of the family and marriage by the intellectuals. People who were happily married were looked down upon as socially stupid and insensitive people. Somehow, misery and trouble were associated with sensitivity in the minds of these intellectuals, and they tended to parade real and pretended griefs and problems as a sign of their superiority.

These attitudes have recurred repeatedly in Western cultures, in the medieval period, the Renaissance, the Enlightenment, and today. The intellectual stance is again one of disdain. The Kinsey reports and other similar ostensibly scientific studies clearly illustrate the intellectual pose. The intellectuals are very clearly anti-family, and they are also on the whole statist. Their answer, not only to the family, but to most human problems, is *love*, love as a panacea, a cure-all. This love can be applied by statist coercion or by individual action, but the answer is, we are told, simply *love*.

This means, as applied to the family, that the family can be legitimately established if love exists, and the family can be broken where love ceases to exist. In saying this, these self-styled leaders are aware that they are weakening the structure of the family, but they make it clear that they do not want the family to exist on anything except this foundation of love. The husband, wife, and children have a right to this magical thing called love.

Now that love has its place in the family and in life generally, the Bible clearly recognizes, but it does not permit love to become so basic to the family or to life. More than love, a family needs a godly law structure, an order, discipline, and security that come from knowing that God's word is paramount in all things. A father or mother may love their child very earnestly, but of what use is that love, and what help, if the father fails to support the child, or is an alcoholic? And of what value is a mother's love for a child if that mother fails to feed the child properly or regularly, or to provide it with the necessary attention, education, and care?

The cocoon in which the child grows and flourishes is a stable home, in which the child's needs for food, clothing, shelter, discipline, teaching, faith, and motivation are conscientiously and faithfully met. It is this that spells love to a child. The Bible says very plainly, "love is the fulfilling of the law" (Rom. 13:10). Love then is more than the sexual passion and the emotional attachment that romanticism talks about. Love is the fulfilling of the law, *God's law.* Thus, when the intellectuals with their shallow thinking offer us love as the foundation of marriage, they are not talking about love but attraction.

Love cannot be separated from the law. Where love truly enters into a marriage, there is a respect for and an obedience to God's law. This means that the marriage is within the faith, with a fellow believer, so that husband and wife are united first of all in terms of a common faith and obedience to God.

Love, in this Biblical sense means, moreover, that the basis of the marriage and of the new family is not personal but Christian. In romantic love, the family is started when romantic feeling draws a man and woman together, and it ends with the death of those feelings. Marriage is thus made a purely personal affair. But the family is a God-given institution and it is the basic social institution. No decision concerning the family therefore can be purely personal. At all times, the family is under God's law, and its beginning and ending must be in terms of obedience to God's law.

This brings us to a very curious fact. These intellectuals are predominantly socialistic, and their approach to most problems is to stress the collective responsibility and the collective answers. But, when they approach religion, morality, marriage, and the family, they tell us that these are purely personal questions, not social or collective problems. Why this curious inconsistency? The answer is that they are by no means inconsistent. Their purpose is to abolish Biblical religion and morality; therefore, they banish it from social life and society by insisting that it is a purely personal and private affair. Similarly, by making the foundation and the grounds of marriage, family, and divorce purely personal, they are in effect destroying the family, since they deny to it its proper social role.

Contempt of the family goes hand in hand with contempt for religion and morality. The breakdown of faith is also the breakdown of the family. The relationship of religion, morality, and the family is a vital one. Whenever statism attacks religion, morality, and the family, it unleashes against them the forces of anarchism. Anarchism thus is the perennial ally of totalitarian statism. The elite who dominate the state are men beyond the law who can govern the world according to their imaginations and concentrate power in their hands to that end. Carle C. Zimmerman, in *Family and Civilization,* has given (p. 639) a telling picture of Homer's world: "The human values common men now prize so highly are nonexistent in Homer. The great in Homer are a few well-born and vigorous freebooters who dominate the rest of society according to their own whims. No important Homeric character is concerned with what becomes of the poor and defenseless masses." The leaders of our day are more sophisticated; they talk about these values even as they gut them; they claim to be the men most concerned over man's plight even as they callously use men to further their own power.

The family can prosper if its foundations be solid, and the true foundation of the family is in Christian faith firmly and solidly grounded in Scripture. And today it is the family which is by-passed and neglected in our education. The family, society's most basic institution, has only a minor part in our education and in our thinking.

But, more than that, for the Bible sex is legitimately associated only with the family, whereas for contemporary thinkers there is a radical separation and dissociation of sex and marriage. For example, in the second Kinsey Report, the family is scarcely mentioned. There is a reference or two to the family at the beginning of one chapter, but only as a prelude to discussing sex, not the family. In the one other reference, we are told that certain "animals travel in family groups or packs," so that the reference is to animals, not to man or the family. This is fairly typical. Today, sex is considered in atomistic and anarchistic isolation from marriage and the family, and this is a deliberate and revolutionary dissociation. There is a deliberate cultivation of anarchistic and atomistic individualism, and it is the anti-family, atomistic individual who is the most congenial to collectivism, because he is at least under law in his own life. Anarchism and totalitarianism are both destructive of law and are triumphs of lawlessness.

The Christian family is basic to God's law order for man. The family is established by God for the welfare and happiness of mankind. The godly family is promised numerous blessings in Scripture: long life, children, prosperity, and much more. According to the Bible, man's truest life is in community, and the God-given community is first of all the family. Psalms 127 and 128 both celebrate the blessedness of godly family life, and many of the Proverbs resound with its praise.

> Behold, that thus shall the man be blessed that feareth the LORD.
> The LORD shall bless thee out of Zion: and thou shalt see the good of Jerusalem all the days of thy life.
> Yea, thou shalt see thy children's children, and peace upon Israel (Ps. 128:4-6).

NINETEEN

JUSTICE AND THE COMMON LAW

Most people are aware of the fact that we are in the midst of what Los Angeles' late Chief of Police Parker called "a legal revolution." The law is no longer held in the same respect; the courts are in process of changing the law by reinterpretation, and the police are under extensive assault in most of the country. These facts, however, are only the aftermath of a legal revolution. The actual revolution in law is already over; we are merely seeing its consequences. About a century ago, the legal revolution began; today, it is being rounded out to its logical completion and consequences.

What was this legal revolution? It was the supplanting of common law as basic to our legal structure and operation with statue law. To understand this, we need to understand what common law means.

First, common law in England and the United States is an age-old doctrine of law, already developing when the medieval period began. Its root is in the Bible. It is the application of the Biblical law and doctrine of justice to the problems of everyday life. Eugen Rosenstock-Huessy has commented,

"Common Law was the product of a union between universal Christian laws and local customs."[1] The common law was the mainstay of the people, Rosenstock-Huessy pointed out: "Common Law was the good law which could not be depreciated by the King's arbitrary power. It did not claim a national origin, but was the dowry of Christian baptism."[2]

This brings us to the *second* point. Common law represented God's law rather than the king's law or the state's law. As a result, the king and the state were under the common law, whereas the king's law sought to put church and people under the king. Henry VIII suppressed the common law as far as possible in order to replace it with his own law. Under common law, supremacy of the law meant that king, state, nor any agency of state was above the law. The Christian had God's common law to appeal to in the courts, and the courts were independent of the state. They were God's ministry of justice, and the law reigned over courts, kings, and people.

A *third* aspect of common law was equally significant. It was not statute law, that is, it was not based upon written laws enacted by an agency of state. The judge based his decision on basic Christian law, Biblical law, and on Biblical doctrines of justice. J. W. Ehrlich, in his analysis, *The Holy Bible and the Law*, cited an 1836 New Hampshire case which the judge decided in terms of the Bible, because common law made such a procedure not only legitimate but basic. This meant that when a crime was committed it was not necessary to find a specific written law to cover the case. The case was always already covered by a basic principle of justice, by Christian principles as adapted to local usage. As a result, the common law had a great deal of flexibility, whereas statute law is very rigid; statue law is governed by the letter of the law rather than by the principle of justice, and legal appeal becomes more an exercise in legal phariseeism than justice.

---

1. Eugen Rosenstock-Huessy, *Out of Revolution: An Autobiography of Western Man* (New York: William Morrow, 1938), 270.
2. Ibid., 271.

Fourth, common law was precedent law. The law of the court was the principle of Christian justice as it had been expressed in judicial decisions. Past decisions provided a ground for deciding present cases, because past decisions were developments of the implications of the basic principle. Now precedent law has remained to a great degree in our legal system in a perverted form. The Supreme Court has used precedent law to overturn historic constitutionalism rather than to further the original concepts of the common law. Moreover, common law, insofar as it exists, has been arrested to include only the common law to 1603, the first year of the reign of James I. Moreover, the central nerve of the common law, the supremacy of God and His law over church, state, and courts, over all man-made laws, has been denied. Without this faith, the common law is essentially a relic rather than a living force. Instead of being the bulwark of the people against injustice, the law today is an esoteric cult whose initiates are only the trained lawyers of the schools. Patrick Henry, for example, was a great lawyer because he represented a great faith and a great moral force, intelligently marshaled and ably disciplined to his task and calling. Today, Patrick Henry's kind of law has no place in the courts, and a different kind of knowledge governs the law.

At the same time, another aspect of our legal revolution has affected the administration of the law. A *fifth* aspect of common law is trial by jury, and this was so basic that the founding fathers felt it necessary, in the First Congress, to meet the popular demand by incorporating it into the Bill of Rights. The Seventh Amendment declares: "In suits at common law, where the value in controversy shall exceed twenty dollars, the right of trial by jury shall be preserved, and no fact tried by a jury shall be otherwise re-examined by any court of the United States than according to the rules of common law." The Constitution thus established both the common law and trial by jury. Trial by jury has a very significant purpose. Among other things, it was intended to preserve the administration of the law to amateurs. The meaning of this was that justice, as administered by the jury, was based, not on a technical knowledge of statute law, but on a Christian sense of justice. A jury made up of the citizens of the community cannot possibly have a lawyer's knowledge of the law. They will obviously be ignorant of the multitude of technicalities which complicate the law. Under common law, the jury simply acted on the basis of its Christian sense of justice and the legal tradition of the community. The jury system is superbly suited to the common law, but it is under attack by the advocates of statute law, statist law, because it is in effect a contradiction. When a vast body of laws and decisions govern the details of a crime, the manner of arrest, the technicalities of presentation in court, then the law is primarily governed by laws of procedure rather than by a Biblical principle of justice. Oliver Wendell Holmes, Jr., in *The Common Law,* saw the common law as basically governed by the motive of "revenge." As a result, he was hostile to the very principles of retribution and responsibility which are basic to justice. His own legal career did much to undermine our common law. We now daily see violations of law and order go unpunished, because our statute law, and its procedural laws, prohibit successful prosecution. Statute law becomes progressively more unwieldy and less enforceable.

Sixth, basic to the common law was the Biblical principle of restitution. Instead of imprisoning a thief, the common law sought to inflict monetary damages on him in order to compensate the victim. Its basic remedy was therefore not imprisonment but restitution, restoring to the offended party damages for his deprivation. As a result, the common law was intensely personal in its orientation. It had as its purpose restoring something to an injured party and penalizing the guilty party in order to do it. In short, the law operated for the welfare of the citizen rather than for the impersonal state and its concept of society.

Statute law, which is not to be confused with a constitution, is the enactment of a legislature. Statute law prevails on the European continent, and it has done much to make

Europe for the past century and more a place of growing statism and of declining liberty. The persistence of the common law in England and the United States made them seem like areas of liberty to the oppressed peoples of Europe. American justice was sometimes rough and crude, but it stood basically for godly liberties, and the peoples of the world were attracted to it. The decline of the common law and the rise of statute law have made for a change in American life and a decline in American liberties. Justice has become a remote concept and the esoteric concern of a group of professionals, and the Supreme Court can make the justice of one day the injustice on the next.

This process is not new. Long ago, the Biblical law was perverted by a class of men into an esoteric doctrine which was beyond the grasp of the people. Our Lord came into immediate conflict with these men, the Pharisees, who made the law of God of none effect with their self-created tradition. The answer to this Phariseeim then and now is the same. Law perishes when the faith which undergirds the law dies. To restore justice, to revive the common law, we need to revive the faith which alone makes it possible. And this is more than a lawyer's concern; it is every man's responsibility before God. And where do you stand before Him?

TWENTY

LANDS WITHOUT JUSTICE

St. Augustine, in his study of society, *The City of God*, made clear how basic to true society justice is. A society which is not grounded on the triune God and His law is a society destined to reveal its basic hostility to justice. As St. Augustine remarked, of the civil turmoil of the Roman republic, "Peace vied with war in cruelty, and surpassed it: for while war overthrew armed hosts, peace slew the defenceless. War gave liberty to him who was attacked, to strike if he could; peace granted to the survivors, not life, but an unresisting death." (Bk. III, 28). Moreover, said Augustine, a nation without justice is no different than a band of robbers. "Justice being taken away, then, what are kingdoms but great robberies? For what are robberies themselves, but little kingdoms?" (Bk IV, 4). Every band of robbers, and every criminal syndicate, Augustine went on to state, has an authority, a head, a body of rules or laws, its own self-policing, its fixed territories and cities, and operates exactly as a nation does. Remove justice from a nation and it has little to distinguish it from a band of robbers or a criminal syndicate.

In order to understand the necessity for justice, it is important to know what the word *justice* means. The dictionary states that justice is the administration or maintenance of that which is just, and the root word, *just*, is defined as *righteous*, so that justice is righteousness. Although dictionaries now tend to play down the religious aspect of the word *righteousness*, it still has, and correctly so, a religious connotation in the popular mind.

In the Bible, righteousness and justice are basically the same words and ideas. Justice and righteousness mean moral and religious perfection, so that God is spoken of as not only perfect righteousness and justice but also as the source of all righteousness and justice. Justice on the human scene means the rule of God's righteousness among men in two ways: *first,* by the operation of divine grace in the heart of man, and, *second,* by means of the ministry of justice through civil government. By means of the state, by civil government, God's righteousness is to be expressed in law, godly law, and the order this law establishes is justice. Take away God's standard of righteousness from the law, and you strip the law of justice and reduce it to anti-law.

Without justice, the law becomes a form of theft. Stripped of justice, the law becomes an instrument of extortion and oppression in the hands of whatever group of men control it. If men of wealth control the state, the law becomes their tool to subjugate the poor and to make them poorer. If poor men control the state, the law then is used to rob the rich and all hardworking men to support those who want to live on the proceeds of robbery. In the one case it is called the maintenance of the social order, and in the other it is called social justice and social welfare, but in both cases it is robbery. And today, because God's righteousness is despised, the nations of the world are becoming robber states and lands without justice.

Humanism has been responsible for creating these robber states. By denying the relevance of God's law to man's law, and by divorcing law from the righteousness of God, humanism has made the law the expression of man's logic and experience. God's higher law is denied, and man becomes the ultimate law and lawgiver. The only difference then between the criminal syndicate and the modern state is that the state claims to have the general will of a nation behind it; the lesser order of the criminal syndicate is thus ruled out as an illegitimate order. But this limited logic could lead a world state to call a national state a criminal order because it merely represents a limited segment of the world's peoples.

Moreover, because humanism has no ultimate right or wrong, its law is democratic law, that is, it simply expresses the will of the people. But the will of man, whether as an individual or en mass, is, according to Scripture, a sinful will. Sinful man is not interested in justice; he is interested in himself, in getting more and more of the best for himself. When man's sinful will is the only source of the law, as it is for humanism, then the law becomes *legalized robbery*, which is, after all, the simplest and best definition of socialism.

With socialism, or legalized robbery, the appetite for robbery is only increased. Men who begin to steal find stealing to be their favored way of progress, and, as a result, theft rather than work becomes steadily more and more basic to the socialistic robber state. Men find it profitable to live by legalized theft, and they demand all the more of it. As a result, while socialism calls itself the *workers' state*, it is in actuality a robbers' state, wherein the robbers live off the workers and insist that the workers thank them for this new paradise! Nowhere are workers more oppressed than under socialism, and yet they are continually asked to hail, praise, and thank the thieves who live off of them.

Lands without justice, robber states, are the consequence of humanism, of a law divorced from God's righteousness. Basic therefore to every resistance to the criminal syndicate states are two things: *first*, personal faith in Christ as Savior, and, *second*, God's righteousness as the foundation of civil order, of law and of justice. Apart from this, we are merely fighting humanism with more humanism, which is comparable to fighting fire with gasoline.

In a land without justice, sympathy tends to favor the unjust rather than the just. As a result, sympathy and pity go out to criminals, not to victims. Every kind of legal protection is increasingly afforded the criminal and less and less to the godly and the law-abiding citizen. We are told that we must love the thief, prostitute, homosexual, and murderer, and that to demand punishment for crimes is to be ugly and vengeful, but little love and pity are shown for the victims of their crimes. We live in one of history's most sentimental eras, and all this sentimentality is lavished upon the hoodlums and criminals of society. In many circles, it is impossible to criticize these hoodlums and criminals without becoming a social outcast. When popular feeling runs so strongly in favor of the lawless, we will always see the progressive growth of a land without justice.

To restore justice, we must restore God to His rightful place in our personal and national lives. For Scripture, true civil governments not only derive their power from God but also their law. According to Scripture, "power belongeth unto God" (Ps. 62:11), and all powers on the human scene can only be exercised according to His word. God "removeth kings, and setteth up kings" (Dan. 2:21), and "the most High ruleth in the kingdom of men, and giveth it to whomsoever he will" (Dan. 4:32). St. Paul stated that "[T]here is no power but of God, the powers that be are ordained of God" (Rom. 13:1). In America, during most of its history, God has been recognized as the source of government by the people and by the courts. At the very beginning, the purpose was openly and proudly stated to be the establishment of godly governments. Thus, the Preamble to the Connecticut Constitution of 1639 declared, "Where a people are gathered together the word of God requires that to maintain the peace and union ... there should be an orderly and decent Government established according to God."

Our courts once agreed with St. Augustine that, "if Justice be taken away, what are governments but great bands of robbers?" Thus, a decision of 1905 stated, "If through the courts of justice, a man can be chiseled out of his property...then it would be well to abolish the courts, and let every man, like the 'heathen rage' and be 'a law unto himself."[1] A decision of 1921 said also, "The right of courts to exist and function rests upon their power to mete out fundamental justice."[2] Where justice is removed from a court, that court simply becomes a political tool whereby one class oppresses another, and justice is replaced by injustice. This, of course, is the theory of Marxist law, for communism uses the law and the courts as a tool for the dictatorship of the proletariat and the oppression of all who in any way oppose, disagree with, or fall out of favor of the totalitarian state.

The Soviet law and courts are the logical end result of humanism and of any legal structure divorced from God's absolute righteousness and justice. "Except the LORD build the house, they labour in vain that build it" (Ps. 127:1).

---

1. Lotta v. Wiley (1905) 92SW433, 437 (Neil, J).
2. State v. Ramirez (1921) 34 Idaho 623, 636, 203P279, 29ALR297 Budge, J.

TWENTY-ONE

THE DEATH OF GOD
AND THE LAW

A new movement with deep roots within the church and in our present humanistic culture is the Death-of-God school of thought. Its leaders are insistent that the God of Scripture, the God of orthodox Christianity, is dead and meaningless. Thomas J. J. Altizer, a leader in this school, has written, in his study of *Mircea Eliade and the Dialectic of the Sacred*, that "God has died in *our* time, in *our* history, in *our* existence. Insofar as we live in our destiny, we can know neither a trace of God's presence nor an image of his reality. We must acknowledge, therefore, that if God has died in our history, then insofar as the church has become Christendom, insofar as the church has entered history, it has become a corpse—as Kierkegaard knew so deeply; and *all* traditional theological meaning, *all* our inherited religious meaning, is in process either of dissolution or of transformation." For Altizer, nothing supernatural can be real, true, or historical; therefore, by definition God cannot exist. According to Altizer, "'historicity' means a total immersion in historical time, an immersion that is totally isolated from any meaning or reality that might lie beyond it." In other words, only that which is completely human is real, and only that which is completely divorced from any supernatural meaning is historical for Altizer. This means that if we believe in God and are governed by His word, by a meaning beyond history, then we are not truly historical, nor do we have historicity!

Altizer, an Episcopalian teaching in a Methodist school, is not alone in his thinking. Leslie Dewart, a Roman Catholic philosopher teaching at St. Michael's College of the University of Toronto, has written on *The Future of Belief.* For Dewart, it is wrong for us to say that God has being, that He exists. The truth about God for Dewart is that He does not exist. Dewart wishes to retain the idea of God without the existence of God, to call the reality-beyond-being but not to allow Him to be real and alive. Dewart wants to talk about God, and he has written a book to tell us what God would have man become, but Dewart's god is by definition a silent god, and therefore Dewart must speak for him!

This is the end result of the Death-of-God school of thought: it gives us a silent god and loud-mouthed philosophers who are the voices of this dead god who is beyond being. The Death-of-God school denies that there is a law founded on God's word, because they deny that God can speak, and the only true world they allow, the voice of historicity, is one wholly immersed in time.

Now these philosophers are quite sure that the voice of true historicity is speaking. In fact, they are quite sure they are speaking for it. The voice of this true historicity, this new god of being, a god who is only human and has no law outside of himself, is best expressed in the modern state. The state becomes the vehicle through which the new god, united humanity, finds itself.

Another leader of the Death-of-God school, William Hamilton, writing on "The Death of God Theology" in *The Christian Scholar*[1] declares that he looks forward to the return of God, but it will not be the God of orthodox Christianity. We must "define Jesus in the world," that is, find Him in the social order in a new world, a united humanity.

The voice of the new god becomes, therefore, the voice of the new man, the purely "historical" man, that is, the man who says there is no God and no law which as any power over him except the law of man. It is a denial of any absolute law, any absolute right and wrong, in the name of pure "historicity," that is, being totally guided by the feelings of the moment and by time.

The modern state is working towards this requirement; it is seeking to be purely "historical" in this existentialist sense. The modern state is denying Christianity and adopting humanistic law. It is affirming itself as the only true source of law. The modern state denies that there is a God whose law is mandatory for all nations, who must be obeyed lest He bring judgment on the nations. The consequence of modern humanism is that the state substitutes itself for God. As Irving Howard observed in *The Christian Alternative to Socialism,* "The exaltation of humanity results in the deification of the personification of man's collective power—government. And so, in our time, the substitution of government for God goes on apace."

The Death-of-God school is in reality a statist school of thought which could be better termed a War-on-God school, because this is its motive and purpose.

Not only true Christianity but also true law is declining in our world today because the roots of this movement are so basic to our culture. They are humanism in its essence, the substitution of man for God as the sovereign and the lawgiver.

The basic fallacy of the Death-of-God school is that its wish is father to its thought. It wants God's death; therefore, He is dead. Unfortunately for them, God is very much alive, and His power undiminished and unchanged. God's law operates in the world in two basic ways, among others. The *first* basic operation of God's law in man's life and world is as *blessing.* If God's

---

1. William Hamilton, "The Death of God Theology," *The Christian Scholar,* Spring, 1965, XLVIII, 1.

law is obeyed, man is blessed. The law then is productive of life to man, because as St. Paul declared, the law "was ordained to life" (Rom. 7:10), and it offers life for the obedient faith, both in time and eternity. We are told that it is God's requirement that we obey, "that thy days may be prolonged, and it may go well with thee, in the land which the LORD thy God giveth thee" (Deut. 5:16). Moreover, the Scripture declares,

> And all these blessings shall come on thee, and overtake thee, if thou shalt hearken unto the voice of the LORD thy God.
>
> Blessed shalt thou be in the city, and blessed shalt thou be in the field.
>
> Blessed shall be the fruit of thy body, and the fruit of thy ground, and the fruit of thy cattle, the increase of thy kine, and the flocks of thy sheep.
>
> Blessed shall be thy basket and thy store.
>
> Blessed shalt thou be when thou comest in, and blessed shalt thou be when thou goest out.
>
> The LORD shall cause thine enemies that rise up against thee to be smitten before thy face: they shall come out against thee one way, and flee before thee seven ways.
>
> The LORD shall command the blessing upon thee in thy storehouses, and in all that thou settest thine hand unto; and he shall bless thee in the land which the LORD thy God giveth thee.
>
> The LORD shall establish thee an holy people unto himself, as he hath sworn unto thee, if thou shalt keep the commandments of the LORD thy God, and walk in his ways.
>
> And all people of the earth shall see that thou art called by the name of the LORD; and they shall be afraid of thee.
>
> And the LORD shall make thee plenteous in goods, in the fruit of thy body, and in the fruit of thy cattle, and in the fruit of thy ground, in the land which the LORD sware unto thy fathers to give thee.
>
> The LORD shall open unto thee his good treasure, the heaven to give the rain unto thy land in his season, and

to bless all the work of thine hand: and thou shalt lend
unto many nations, and thou shalt not borrow.

And the LORD shall make thee the head, and not the tail;
and thou shalt be above only, and thou shalt not be be-
neath; if that thou hearken unto the commandments of
the LORD thy God, which I command thee this day, to
observe and to do them:

And thou shalt not go aside from any of the words which I
command thee this day, to the right hand, or to the left,
to go after other gods to serve them. (Deut. 28:2-14)

This, then, is the first major form whereby God's law is operative in the world, by *blessings*.

The *second* major form of God's operative law is *cursing*.
God curses and blights every disobedient person and people
and brings them to judgment. According to Scripture,

But it shall come to pass, if thou wilt not hearken unto the
voice of the LORD thy God, to observe to do all his commandments and his statutes which I command thee this
day; that all these curses shall come upon thee, and over-
take thee:

Cursed shalt thou be in the city, and cursed shalt thou be
in the field.

Cursed shall be thy basket and thy store.

Cursed shall be the fruit of thy body, and the fruit of thy
land, the increase of thy kine, and the flocks of thy
sheep.

Cursed shalt thou be when thou comest in, and cursed
shalt thou be when thou goest out. (Deut. 28:15-19)

Most people fight shy of the idea of a curse, but it is impossible to bless without cursing. To reward righteousness
requires punishing evil. And the true God is the God of Scripture, the God of our Lord Jesus Christ, the God who blesses
and curses. And He shall prevail, "the same yesterday, today,
and for ever" (Heb. 13:8). The real question is not as to
whether God is alive or dead, but rather, it concerns ourselves.
Where do we stand in terms of His word, law, grace, and
calling? Under blessings, or curses?

MARXIST LAW

The Marxist doctrine of law is a major force in the twentieth century. For Marx and Lenin, the basic fact is seen as the denial of truth. Marxism is relativistic; it denies that there is any absolute truth, any fundamental right and wrong in the universe. Instead of God as the source of truth and law, Marxism insists that all ideas of truth and law simply reflect the will of a ruling class. Thus, for communism, law is simply the will of the ruling class stated as statues and legal requirements, so that the law merely mirrors the policies of the ruling class as it operates through the state. As a result, for Marxism there is no truth in any law; no law has any relationship to any absolute right and wrong, because no absolute right or wrong exists. This means that Communist law is no more true than capitalistic law; that is, that Soviet law and Red China's laws are no more true in any absolute sense than the U. S. Constitution. The only difference the Marxists make is this: the Constitution supposedly represents, not the people, but the will of a capitalistic ruling class, whereas Marxist law is more democratic; it supposedly represents the will of the proletariat. And,

since Marxism is economic humanism, man is its only standard of value; therefore, the will of the proletariat is relatively
better than the will of the capitalists, because there are more
proletarians in the world. Albert Weisbord, a prominent
Marxist, attacked the U. S. Constitution, not because it was
true or false, but because he believed it to be anti-democratic,
anti-proletarian, and in his study, *The Conquest of Power,* he saw
the Constitutional Convention of 1787 as a part of "a secret
conspiracy" against the people (Vol. I, p. 71). The Constitution, of course, asserted implicitly the supremacy of the law
over all classes and peoples, and, as Edward S. Corwin has
pointed out, it presupposed a "higher law," the law of God.[1]
But, for Marxism, all talk about God and God's law is a façade
and sham used by a ruling class to suppress the poor.

For Marxism, law is simply the will of the state. It has no
reference to any absolute right or wrong, nor is there any
higher law than the state. Law is simply a system of prescriptive
and binding rules which express the totalitarian and coercive
will of the state. This Marxist theory was developed further by
Andrey Vishinsky, who applied his theory both as the Soviet
prosecutor in the great purge trials of the 1930s, and again as
the head of the Soviet delegation to the United Nations. For
Vyshinskiy, and as a result for the Communist states, law is a
weapon to be used against the enemy in the fight for socialism
and an instrument for reconstructing human society on a
socialist basis. It is thus a political tool.

From this, two things have already become apparent. *First,*
Marxist law denies any absolute truth, any ultimate right and
wrong, and *second,* law is a political weapon to be used in
destroying enemies and remaking its subjects.

A *third* aspect of Marxist law is equally evident. It is summed
up in the slogan of the Soviet system: "All power belongs to the
Soviets." This is totalitarianism, the dictatorship of the proletariat. Communism is not opposed to totalitarianism as such. It

---

1. Edward S. Corwin, *The "Higher Law" Background of the American Constitutional Law,* 1928 (Ithaca: Cornell, 1955).

is merely opposed to all non-Communist totalitarian states, but it is definitely in favor of its own form of totalitarianism.

A *fourth* aspect of Marxist law is its use of the courts. Since the law has no reference to an absolute right and wrong, neither can the courts be geared to any absolute justice. The courts have nothing to do with justice; they simply safeguard the interests of the Soviet state and work to destroy all its enemies. The courts therefore cannot tolerate any appeal to absolute justice. They move in terms of what is called "Soviet justice," that is, the will of the state.

Fifth, as is clearly apparent, Soviet law does not tolerate any division of powers, because it is by its own definition totalitarian. As a result, the courts have no independence. Lenin and Vishinsky insisted that the courts, like the army, and the administration of the state as a whole, have one function, to further socialism and destroy its enemies.

Sixth, Marxism denies that anything can be called law which does not further socialism. As a result, all Christian systems of law are called frauds, because by definition law is the correct action of the socialist state. As a result, it works to discredit every other law system and to bring about its breakdown in order to replace it with socialist, with revolutionary "justice," that is, the destruction of capitalists, churches, independent groups, and all things hostile to communism.

Seventh, this means that for Marxists the only real crimes are crimes against socialism, that is, opposition to Marxist totalitarianism. New crimes are accordingly invented, and we now hear the term "crimes against peace" freely used. A crime against peace is any kind of war against Marxism. It is a new and dangerous concept, because it involves a faith that Marxism is the one true god, and any opposition to it is a mortal sin. There has been no change in this Marxist concept; it has only been developed more fully. The only real complaints against Stalin by his successors were for offenses to ruling Marxists, not for his offenses against true justice. Milovan Djilas, in his book *Conversations With Stalin*, said, "As long as Stalin's successors are mourning, on the one hand, individual victims of arbitrary rule between 1937 and 1955 but do not talk on the other hand about the millions of victims of Bolshevik persecution among the peasants, the middle classes, and the Russian intelligentsia, we cannot believe them that they have turned away honestly and sincerely from the methods of violent oppression and of terror."

This brings us to an *eighth* aspect of the Soviet system of law. Because it is totalitarian and political law, it insures a perpetual state of civil war. In fact, it creates a double civil war. First, it creates a civil war within the ruling Communists. The Soviet Union has seen a long civil war, first, between Lenin's successors, next, between Stalin's successors, and the present scene is far from a quiet one. The Communists of Red China are in the midst of a civil war between the ruling assassins, and the triumph of one party or another will not end the trouble. The second kind of civil war created by Marxist law is between the state and the people, and the state wars against its own people as an enemy. Because the Communist state always regards its subjects as an enemy either to be remade by brainwashing and brute force, or to be crushed by terror and violence, peace between the party and the people is an impossibility. Because the Soviet state is the totalitarian and absolute power, it can do no wrong, and the people are therefore by definition wrong if they do not submit totally to the state. Moreover, the people are also in the wrong even if they do submit. When communism makes a mistake, it refuses to accept guilt, because it is by definition the perfect system. Someone must be made the scapegoat, and the scapegoat becomes either portions of the Communist Party, or else the people, or both. That someone must then be punished. As a result, communism, because it is not nor can be perfect or free from failures, must with every failure make civil war against itself and its people. This means that communism can never bring peace, because its Marxist theory of law guarantees perpetual war and the destruction of that which law is supposed to ensure—justice and order.

Now no society can exist without law, and when a system of law turns out to be anti-law, it ensures that instead of society there will be anarchy and chaos. The Webbs called the Soviet Union a new civilization; instead of a new civilization, it is a sorry substitute for civilization, civil war instead of culture. Instead of the rule of law, it substitutes the rule of terror and of brute force. In the name of man, in the name of humanism, Marxism claims to offer mankind a new hope to replace Christian revelation.[2] What it offers instead is the worst horrors of humanity's experience and unrelieved terror and perpetual civil war. It is the logic of humanism carried to its conclusion, and its logic is suicidal. As our Lord, speaking as Wisdom, said long ago: "He that sinneth against me wrongeth his own soul: all they that hate me love death" (Prov. 8:36).

---

2. Hermann Raschhofer, *Political Assassination* (Tubenjen: Fritz Schlichten-mayer, 1964).

TWENTY-THREE

THE ABSURDITY OF
PARENTHOOD TODAY

An article by Sid Ross in *Parade*, February 26, 1967, stated its case in the title: "The big change in adoptions: babies can't get parents." According to Ross, the most desirable babies now cannot receive adoption, because there is so great a decline in couples desiring to adopt babies. As a result, the San Diego County welfare department, and many other similar agencies, finds itself with an increasing number of babies and a decreasing ratio of adopting parents. The Child Welfare League of America has reported that in five years the number of children available for adoption has increased 44.5 percent, while the number of applications has increased only 27 percent.

But this is not all. The birth rate is dropping alarmingly all over the world. While the propagandists talk about a population explosion, the reality is a plunging decline in birth rate all over the world. In California, in one of the better areas birth-rate-wise, hospitals have recorded a one-third to one-half drop in births in the past three years, and more maternity divisions are now losing money. At the present rate, we will soon have a

statewide surplus of schoolrooms when the decreased birth
rate hits the schools. The plain fact is that there is a serious
population decline, and, in some parts of the world, as in
Vienna, Austria, the death rate is double the birth rate. Two-
thirds of the nations of Europe are failing even to reproduce
their present adult population.

There is no great reason to be surprised at all this. The
most effective birth control in all history is in operation today,
and it is *not* the pill, nor anything medical. It is the law. The
law today penalizes parents at every turn and discourages
responsible parenthood.

If you are a parent, this is what you face: you are the guilty
party if your child gets into trouble. If a child becomes delinquent, it is because the parents failed in their responsibility,
we are told. If the child's academic performance is poor, then
the parents are accused of failing to motivate the child. At
every turn, the law denies the Biblical doctrine of personal
responsibility and holds to environmentalism. The parents are
the environment of the child, and therefore they are held to
be responsible. They have not done enough for the child, or
loved the child enough. The result is that on every turn there
are legal and social inducements to juvenile irresponsibility.
Since the child is already a sinner by nature, these inducements provide opportunities for the development of the
child's sinful nature. It is no wonder that the child becomes a
spoiled monster.

On top of this, there are financial penalties to being a
parent. It is an expensive thing today to rear a child, to feed
and clothe it, to place it in a Christian school, provide for a college education, and maintain a home large enough to house
a family. The annual expense is very high when all these factors are considered. But the tax benefit is a $600 exemption
annually. Even more than the pill, the law today discourages
parenthood.

But this is not all. The parents support the child today for
eighteen years, if the child quits school after high school

graduation, but, increasingly, the support extends on through junior college, college, and even graduate school. It is no exaggeration to say that each child receives an average of twenty years of support. But the help does not end there. When the child marries, the support very often continues in direct and indirect ways. In many cases, the parents help provide employment, furniture, or other items, but, without this, the support is still considerable. Consider, for example, the number of grandparents whose week is regularly tied to some babysitting, or who do all the babysitting for their children's vacation. Consider also the number of grandmothers who babysit while their daughters go to work to increase the family's income, and also the number of grandparents who have taken over the children temporarily or permanently because of divorce. Add to this the cost of presents regularly, for two or three children, their husbands and wives, and all the grandchildren. Most grandparents find they must keep a datebook for all the birthdays, anniversaries, graduations, and the like in their family.

The result is that parents give full support to a child for a good twenty years, and partial support for another thirty years, for a half a century. Then, perhaps in their declining years, the father or mother, or both, need help because inflation has wiped out their savings, or long, serious illnesses have drained both their finances and their health, and they need physical care and financial help. How many can go to their children? Most parents say, "I would never want to." What they too often mean is that they don't want to be humiliated by the children's reluctance to help.

This whole picture adds up to one fact: the absurdity of parenthood today. Our legal framework has made it absurd. Love does not flourish, nor health develop, under a condition of parasitism. If someone is a continual parasite on someone, perpetually receiving and never giving, always asking but never repaying, that person is hardly likely to be loved. When the law allows children to become parasites, then the law is working to destroy the natural relationship of parent and child. In a normal family, the child needs the parents much of his life, and then the parents need the children, and unless the relationship works both ways, it is a sick one and is socially destructive. It leads to a false independence on the part of parents, and to a false dependence on the part of children. Parents who need to rely now on their children refuse to do so and make foolish decisions, and children who need to care for their parents stand around coldly waiting to divide whatever inheritance there may be. Is it any wonder that many are refusing to be parents under these conditions? Parenthood today is an absurdity by law; the child is a legally protected parasite.

Not only is the child made a lifelong parasite, but our society makes adolescence a legitimate form of insanity. We have come to associate adolescence with rebelliousness and emotionalism, and we consider this to be naturally a time of stress in a person's life. But this is not true of every culture, nor was it once true of our own. Adolescence has often been in history a particularly proud and happy age, the time of maturity. It is a mentally sick and spiritually sinful adolescence that wants independence while being subsidized by the parents.

The answer to these problems is very clearly established in Scripture. The children are commanded, not asked, to *honor* their father and mother. Notice the form of the commandment; children are not asked to *love* their parents, but they are required at all times to *honor* them, and, until they establish their own homes, to *obey* their parents (Deut. 5:16; Eph. 6:1–3). This is not made a matter of choice; it is a matter of law. Children are not asked by God to love their parents, nor parents to love their children; love cannot be commanded, and, even more basic than love is obedience to God and to God's commandments. Parents *must* bring up their children "in the nurture and admonition of the Lord," St. Paul tells us (Eph. 6:4), and nurture means discipline, and admonition means commandments. The commandment is "obey your parents in the Lord: for this is right" (Eph. 6:1), that is, it must be God-centered, God-ordered obedience, not a humanistic one.

But this is not all. Our Lord made clear that a gift to God was not acceptable or holy if it meant denying one's parents of their due care. He denounced the Pharisees and scribes for countenancing such a thing: "[Y]e suffer him no more to do ought for his father or his mother; Making the word of God of none effect through your tradition" (Mark 7:12–13). St. Paul declared that "if any provide not for his own, and specially for those of his own house, he hath denied the faith, and is worse than an infidel" (1 Tim. 5:8). By this Paul meant that parents have an obligation to care for their own, which means both their children and the grandparents also, as need may require. This does not say that grandparents are duty-bound to receive help, or to live with their children; it does say that their needs, as they arise, must be met by their children, and that this is a requirement by God. Failure to meet this requirement is a denial of the faith, and, more than that, Paul declares, makes one "worse than an infidel," a consummate hypocrite and denier of the faith.

The Bible's language here is very blunt, and with reason, because a departure from this law means a departure from Christian social order. It means the enthronement of a self-centered psychology and the destruction of family life. Instead of being a blessing, children become a curse. Instead of maturity, they develop into full-fledged parasites, who sponge on their parents and create a socialist society. Socialism is simply a social order which attempts to take over the functions of the family and provide cradle-to-grave security which is the function of the family. In order to have socialism, there must be a population of spoiled children who want a great father who can provide them with more than their parents can, take their parents off their hands, and protect them from the necessity of growing up. Whenever and wherever the family breaks down, socialism results as the substitute for the family. But socialism destroys itself, because it cannot truly replace the family, and, unless the family reestablishes its godly order, the result is chaos. There are no shortcuts to liberty and maturity. The godly family is basic to a free country.

TWENTY-FOUR

CUSTOM AND MORALITY

Customs or social mores govern us often much more strongly than does morality. Most people are more afraid of offending their friends through bad taste than of offending God by sin. Girls who think nothing of disobeying God and their parents will actually weep over the thought of facing their friends with an old dress.

There is an old story of a girl some few years back who, facing the possibility of a cold and working in a drafty office, was persuaded to go to work wearing some old-fashioned and heavy underwear. At the close of the day, she accepted a dinner engagement with a businessman who stopped by, went to his hotel room with him with no hesitancy, and then, suddenly remembering her underwear, fought like a tigress to prevent events from taking their expected course. It was not sin she dreaded, but being seen with old-fashioned underwear.

This illustration points up an important social reality. In every age there are many to whom appearance is more important than morality, but, when an age is dominated and controlled by such a disposition, the result is a rapid social decline. Morality requires faith and courage. It means making a stand and taking a course in terms of God's reality rather than man's reality. Morality in a sinful world places a man in tension with that world at the very least, and potentially in direct opposition to it. The moral man is governed by God and his conscience, and as a result, he is more inclined to be independent of the group and self-reliant in relationship to society. Morality is productive of godly individualism and independence of spirit.

Where custom rules, however, a contrary spirit prevails. People become group-directed, and they feel it imperative to be members of the pack. Their standards vary as the customs and fads of the group vary. Instead of being individualistic, they are collectivistic, anxious at all times to be with a particular group whose customs are their social code. Society then is governed by mob psychology, by the law of the pack, and the social order lacks stability or character.

Today custom rather than morality governs our world, and our politics is the politics of the pack. The accepted social image must be met, or a man, however good his character and qualifications, has little chance for office. Abraham Lincoln receives almost worship from people today, but only because he is a century away. His high-pitched voice would get only ridicule and laughter from today's voters, and many of his personal mannerisms would rule him out of consideration for any office. We have become savagely intolerant of harmless mannerisms and physical conditions which are not approved of by the pack, and at the same time, we regard as unimportant the essentials of morality. Men have been reelected to public office repeatedly after clear-cut evidence of their immorality and misconduct of office. Sometimes their misconduct has even enhanced their popularity.

This attitude is no less prevalent in the churches. Let us examine a specific and typical case. A very prominent, talented, and handsome minister of a very important church was repeatedly guilty of dishonesty. Although it was well known that he said whatever pleased people, without regard for the truth or another man's reputation, no one thought ill of him for this, and his popularity only increased. He was, moreover, far from believing all that he preached and professed to believe, and this, too, was known, and yet he continued to flourish. Then, quite suddenly, his wife died and left him with three small children. He was totally helpless in caring for them. One of his wife's relatives, who came to the funeral, saw his plight and stayed to help him. About six months later they married, since the man obviously needed her and had come to love her, and maintaining two homes was a financial drain. In a very real sense, this marriage was one of the few commendable acts in this minister's life. But he lost his pastorate because of it, because the members were outraged that he did not wait a year before remarrying! Custom was to them more important than morality. Some members made it clear that they would have been indulgent of sexual irregularities during that year, but an open flouting of custom they held to be unforgivable!

Wherever a society places custom above morality, there a revolutionary situation exists. When custom is more important than morality, the first step toward revolution has been taken. The moral foundations of the social order have been denied, and a revolution in standards and behavior has taken place. As a result, an important thrust of all subversive activity is the undermining of morality. Where morality has been undermined, law and religion have also been undermined, so that the major task of revolution has been accomplished. A revolution cannot readily succeed where the existing order has moral vitality, but a revolution is virtually accomplished where moral order has been destroyed.

Moral order represents the establishment on earth of objective ethical or moral truth; it is the conformity of earth and man to the will and word of God. Moral order establishes society in more than itself; it grounds society in truth and thereby makes possible the health and welfare of society as a whole, and it provides the best possible framework for the liberty and development of man.

Customs, mores, or folkways are merely the conventions of a people. Sometimes they are helpful; at other times, they are not only a hindrance but a menace, especially when they govern a people. It is socially and personally advantageous for people to be concerned about their appearances. It makes for greater cleanliness, attractiveness, and social courtesy. Such customs and conventions have their place, but it must be a subordinate one. When appearance becomes more important than morality, then social decadence prevails, and society is in the midst of revolution.

The greatest asset to any revolutionary group is a large body of people who are governed by conventions or customs. With such people, since appearance is all that matters, the country can be gutted of its historical position, constitutionalism, and liberties, and there will be no objection as long as the form is retained. The same is true of their church relationships; they do not ask that their church be truly Christian, but only that it retain the form of being Christian. Their church can deny the faith every Sunday, teach their children the new morality, abandon its confession of faith, maintain through its missionary programs a revolutionary campaign and these people will never leave. They will maintain a façade of being Christian by complaining indignantly about some of the most flagrant activities of their church and clergy, but they will never leave. And rightly so, because they belong there: the dead among the dead. These people who cling to the appearance rather than the reality are the bread and butter of all revolutionary groups; they finance them, support them, and defend them, because they too are revolutionists. They are in revolt against moral order, and they substitute conventional order in its place. They are the first wave of every revolution, and, even though the second wave first uses them and then destroys them, the conventional people are still part of the revolution.

This means we cannot treat people who sit complacently in apostate churches, and who ignore all subversion in the

political order, simply as blind people. They are themselves
the first great wave of social revolution, of moral anarchy and
national and religious decadence. They are more deadly,
these conventional people, than the organized revolutionists,
because their position is more contagious and more destructive. There is, after all, a measure of honesty about an out and
out revolutionist. He knows what he is, and he makes sure that
you also are aware of it. He issues his manifestoes and tells the
world what he plans to do.

But the conventional people have a deadlier revolution.
They approach Christianity and they bury it under their mass
of conventions and forms. They are for the Bible, but it
doesn't really mean what it says, and we mustn't go overboard
on these things. They believe in Christ, but only in terms of a
sensibly modern perspective, of course, and so on. They retain
the form of Christianity and the church, but totally deny the
faith in actuality. They replace reality with their conventions.

The conventional people treat all subversive movements
the same way. They are always certain the Communists, like
Jesus, mean exactly what any sensible conventional person
thinks. They no more take the Communists of their terms
than they take Jesus Christ on His terms. Whatever the Communists said yesterday has no meaning today; they are bound
to change and become just like us! When I was a boy, Stalin,
we were told, represented a conservative reaction against
Trotsky. When I was in college, I was assured that, since Stalin
was purging the old Bolsheviks, capitalism would soon return
to the Soviet Union. And now we are treated to the same old
chant: the Communists are changing!

The reason of course is this: the conventional people,
having substituted appearance for reality, customs for moral
order, cannot face reality in any direction. They cannot see
God as God, nor Satan as Satan. They recognize neither good
nor evil, only appearances. Nothing else is real for them. All
people are exactly like themselves, or they are mentally sick.
Conventional people are only blind in the sense that they are

self-consciously, deliberately, and passionately averse to facing reality. They are like the people of whom Isaiah spoke, who, hearing will not hear, and seeing will not see, lest their minds understand, and their health be restored (Isa. 6:10–11). The destiny of such people is then to be blinded by God and led to destruction. Their nature and destiny is death. Our nature and destiny in Jesus Christ is righteousness and life.

TWENTY-FIVE

THE ANNIVERSARY
OF COMMUNISM

In 1967, the Soviet Union celebrated the 50th anniversary of the socialist revolution of 1917. Communist publications hailed that event and its anniversary as important dates in the history of mankind. Lenin in particular was singled out for great praise as the leader of that revolution. In fact, today Leninism is the approved form whereby Marxism is to be understood. It is important for us, therefore, to examine Lenin's thinking.

The man Lenin was a dedicated admirer of the murderous Nechayev, who advocated the use of total terror, lies, murder, and any means possible to obtain the revolutionary objective. Lenin also commended Petr Tkachev, a similar degenerate, and he urged everyone to read him. The strategy of these men was to offer the peasants every kind of desirable property and life in order to stimulate revolution and without anything but contempt for the people. Lenin believed in dictatorship; "equal rights" was a phrase to be used to catch fools. After the Revolution, in 1920, Lenin declared, "All phrases about equal rights are nonsense."

On November 17, 1917, Lenin declared, "We will destroy everything and on the ruins we will build our temple! It will be a temple for the happiness of all. But we will destroy the entire bourgeoisie, grind it to a powder ... I will be merciless with all counter-revolutionists." According to Lenin, human nature craves submission, requires dictatorship. His purpose was to establish total dictatorship and use total power to remake man and the world. Lenin therefore justified violence and oppression. He suppressed not only all hostile, monarchistic newspapers and periodicals, but he also suppressed all rival Marxist publications. He justified this by declaring, November 17, 1917, "To tolerate those papers is to cease to be a Socialist ... The state is an institution built up for the sake of exercising violence. Previously this violence was exercised by a handful of money-bags over the entire people; now we want ... to organize violence in the interests of the people." Although Lenin talked publicly about democracy at times, yet after a meeting on January 19, 1918, Lenin told Trotsky, "The dissolution of the Constituent Assembly by the Soviet Government means a complete and frank liquidation of the idea of democracy by the idea of dictatorship."

Lenin advocated total terror as the means of destroying all opposition—wholesale murder, destruction, and unremitting violence. He saw mercy as a bourgeois virtue, and one of his common remarks was, "There are no morals in politics; there is only expedience." Morality was for him nonsense, and he declared, to a gathering of Young Communists, "We repudiate all morality which proceeds from supernatural ideas or ideas which are outside class conceptions. In our opinion, morality is entirely subordinate to the interests of class war. Everything is moral which is necessarily for the annihilation of the old exploiting social order and for uniting the proletariat. Our morality, then, consists solely in close discipline and in conscious war against the exploiters. We do no believe in external principles of morality and we will expose this deception. Communist morality is identical with the fight for strengthening the dictatorship of the proletariat." Of religion, Lenin said,

"Religion is the opiate of the people, a sort of spiritual liquor, meant to make the slaves of capitalism drown their humanity and their desires for a decent existence."[1]

When the Bolsheviks seized power, Lenin, in an article entitled "Will the Bolsheviks Retain State Power?" declared that his program was a success precisely because the Bolshevik seizure of power was so widely detested: "We hear the voice of approbation, not in the dulcet sounds of praise, but in the roar of irritation!" Since everyone else was by definition the enemy, whatever displeased the enemy had to be good to Lenin.

In the same article, Lenin described the necessary ingredients for a revolution. An insurrection requires, he said, *first,* "the maturing of the revolution on a general national scale." This means that across the nation not a majority but a sizable and active element must come to believe that their only real hope is in revolutionary violence. They must regard all lawful measures as a subterfuge and snare, as an attempt to fool the masses into being inactive and subservient. Thus, the first ingredient of revolution is a number of people whose hope and activity is violence and terror. *Second,* the "complete moral and political collapse of the old." Notice that Lenin placed moral collapse ahead of political collapse. In order to make this collapse possible, everything was done prior to the Russian Revolution to assault, ridicule, and deny the religious and moral foundations of the nation. People will not fight to preserve something that is meaningless to them. Hence, by every means possible, the spiritual, moral, and political heritage of a people must be made meaningless to them. This involves an assault on a people's religion and education, to make them means of undercutting their intellectual and spiritual roots and reducing them to a position of nihilism. The *third* necessary ingredient for revolution, Lenin declared, is "great vacillation among all the intermediate elements, i.e., among those who are *not* fully in favour of the government, although they fully supported it yesterday." This point is a critical one: "great

---

1. *See* David Shub, *Lenin* (New York: Mentor, 1950).

vacillation," the inability to make a strong stand. Create revolutionarily violence among a people in moral and political collapse, and they will tend increasingly to respond with moral vacillation, unable to make a strong stand. Instead of dealing firmly with violence, they will appease it. Instead of condemning violence, they will excuse it. These morally nerveless and broken men will deny they are for violence and revolution, but they will also refuse to make a clear-cut stand against it. They become thereby a great asset to any revolutionary element and a necessary ingredient for revolution.

Lenin's analysis is an excellent one. It is hardly necessary to add that we have all three ingredients of revolution in our midst today—the revolutionary activity and violence, the moral and political collapse developing, and the great vacillation and inability to make a clear-cut stand dominating our contemporary world scene, as well as the home front.

Lenin advocated violence and terror, not a reasoned, dispassionate program. However, this violence had to be planned violence. He liked Karl Marx's statement that "the armed 'uprising, like war, is an art.'" He cited Marx's chief rules for armed uprisings, which Lenin called "a *special* kind of political struggle." *First*, "Never *play* at uprising, but once it is begun, remember firmly that you have *to go to the very end.*" *Second*, "It is necessary to gather *a great preponderance of forces* in a decisive place at a decisive moment, else the enemy, being in a position of better preparation and organization, will annihilate the insurgents." *Third*, "Once the uprising has been begun, one must act with the greatest decisiveness, one must take the offensive, absolutely, and under all circumstances. 'Defense is the death of an armed uprising.'" *Fourth*, "One must strive to take the enemy by surprise, to take advantage of a moment when his troops are scattered." *Fifth*, "One must try daily for at least small successes (one may even say hourly, when it is a question of one city), thus maintaining under all circumstances a 'moral superiority.'" Marx and Lenin both emphasized Danton's statement, "Audacity, more audacity, and still more audacity." Practically applied, Lenin meant by these principles that communication media should first be seized—telephone exchanges, railway stations, telegraph offices, and bridges. Today, power plants would be added to this list. Isolate a city by these steps, Lenin said, and then move on to the various centers. The "watchword," Lenin said, "must be; *Let all die, but do not allow the enemy to pass.*"[2]

A very important point emerges from all of this. From the standpoint of Western parliamentarians, Communist tactics are crude and bungling. These Westerners are sure that the Communists will mature and outgrow their inept ways, because they equate maturity with parliamentarianism and immaturity with violence. Moreover, because the goal of Western politics is to *persuade, not to coerce*, they insist on seeing the Communist tactics as poor public relations, as an inability to persuade. But, to the Communists, this Western parliamentarianism is the ridiculous and immature political approach. Violence, they hold, is more successful and more logical, given their philosophy of history. Moreover, the Communists are not interested in persuading; their goal is to coerce. Their record of coercion is highly successful; why should they turn now to persuasion?

From the perspective of Lenin, the struggle between capitalism and communism is *total war*. The strategy he therefore demanded was the strategy of total warfare. This strategy was all the easier for him because he held morality to be a myth. The strategy of total warfare becomes all the easier if your enemy falls prey to delusions and is the victim of wishful thinking, and believes that he is on a debating platform instead of a battlefield. This delusion can be encouraged to make the task of destruction easier. Where warfare develops, the Communist screams about his enemies' "atrocities" in a limited war, and at the same time wages total war.

The result of Lenin's realism has been a high degree of Communist success. One of the central features of Lenin's system is consistency and single-mindedness, a total dedication

---

2. "Advice from an Outsider," Lenin, *Collected Works* II (New York, International Publishers, 1932), 97–98.

to one purpose. Leninism cannot be fought by men who mistake war for negotiations and a battle for a debate, and who cannot recognize when and where they are being attacked. The Western liberal pays lip service to a few Christian ideas, holds to a Marxist environmentalism, and an English parliamentarianism. Like the mule, he is a hybrid, and just as sterile. The future can never be commanded by men who cannot command the present. The times call for Christian faith and realism; nothing less can command the day.

TWENTY-SIX

Nepotism and the Law

Periodically, year in and year out, articles appear in magazines and newspapers attacking nepotism. The word nepotism has an insidious sound; it suggests criminality and vice, and it carries an unpleasant connotation. Actually, the original meaning of nepotism was favoritism to nephews in hiring, and the word has come to mean favoritism to any relative in hiring, especially in civil government.

The subject of nepotism is rarely considered fairly or unemotionally. A typical treatment is Jack Anderson's "Let's Kick Relatives Off Congressional Payrolls," in *Parade*. Anderson cites a variety of congressional cases: a congressman whose wife is his secretary, others who hire uncles, brothers, cousins, and, in one case, even a mother-in-law. Nepotism, Anderson tells us sadly, is a bipartisan practice, and, he concludes: "Public confidence in Congress is so low that the legislators should wipe out even the suspicion of wrong-doing. The time has come to outlaw nepotism." [1]

---

1. Jack Anderson, "Let's Kick Relatives Off Congressional Payrolls," *Parade,* February 19, 1967, 6f.

Anderson's article is written with a note of strong moral indignation, and Anderson quite obviously believes himself to be championing the cause of reform. The question needs to be raised, however, very earnestly and urgently, as to whether Anderson's moral perspective is not radically wrong. More than that, the whole question of nepotism needs to be reviewed: is it really a morally questionable practice? Is there a defense possible for nepotism on the highest possible moral grounds? Is it possible that the idea that nepotism represents an immoral practice is itself indicative of a radical moral decline?

Anderson's report is morally wrong, because, first of all, it makes no moral distinction between fraud and honest work. The case of a congressman's wife is cited, who earned $20,288.46 a year without working. "Her most urgent business with his congressional office had been a request for instructions in Spanish or how to play dominoes." This clearly is a case of fraud, and it should be treated as such. Money so received is morally to be regarded as theft. We can all agree that such a practice must be condemned, but it must also be insisted that to equate such fraud with the honest work of a relative is also morally wrong. The congressman or senator who hires a relative—son, daughter, or mother-in-law—and from his relative receives faithful and honest work, cannot be equated with a man who defrauds the government. To make this equation is a sign of moral delinquency. Second, Anderson's article never raises the all-important question: what is wrong with nepotism? Is there anything wrong with hiring a relative to work for you, in government or business, if that relative gives good and faithful service?

To understand the moral issues involved in nepotism, let us examine its history very briefly. The word nepotism was coined several centuries ago to describe the practice of various popes of hiring their nephews to fulfill important roles in the Vatican and in the Papal States. The practice gained especial prominence under Pope Nicholas III toward the close of the thirteenth century; it was also very severely criticized as part of the practice of Sixtus VI in the fifteenth century. The Borgia pope,

Alexander VI, was also notorious for his nepotism. The practice was finally outlawed by Popes Innocent XI and XII in the seventeenth century. There is no doubt that some of the scandals connected with some relatives gave both nepotism and the church a bad name, but it seems hardly likely that Alexander VI would have been any better morally had he not practiced nepotism. Not all popes practiced nepotism for corrupt reasons; most had important considerations in mind. They needed the confidential help of someone of unquestioned loyalty, who would enable them to execute their plans of action without betrayal or hesitation. Only a relative could give this kind of loyalty, and hence the use of relatives. Where the plan of action was morally sound, there was no harm and much good in the use of trustworthy men. Where a program is morally unsound, it makes no difference who is used to execute it.

The situation of congressmen and senators is very similar. They are exceedingly vulnerable to bad public relations, a bad press, infiltration by interests subversive of their own purposes and of their office, and the bribing of confidential secretaries and aides is a commonplace fact of business administration and well as in the administration of offices in the civil government. Under such circumstances, a man's most trustworthy associates are the members of his family; they have an honest vested interest in protecting him in the discharge of his duties. It is true that this may mean that two, three, or four, or five salaries will go to a man and his relatives, but, as long as it is for work honestly done, there is no moral wrong in this practice. It is often a necessary safeguard and security measure, basic to a sound administration of office.

Similarly, in the business world, many a man makes room in his office for relatives, or for his sons. And why not? If his relatives fail to do their work properly, it is he who suffers for it, business-wise. Similarly, if a congressman's wife proves to be a poor secretary and offends the public, the congressman is the loser.

But we have not touched on the basic moral issue as yet. Why this strange belief that the employment of a member of the family is morally wrong? In the medieval church, the criticism came in part from the monastic hostility to the family; it was assumed that a churchman should be dead to the world and to his family. In the modern world, there is an even more anti-family motive at work. Inheritance taxes, income taxes, property laws, and other legislation have worked to limit the independence and authority of the family. The family has less and less rights and less and less independence. Instead of assuming that a man's best helpers are the members of his family, it is assumed that there is some moral wrong in having family help. Articles such as Anderson's attack responsible men and classify them with men guilty of fraudulent practices, simply because they rely on family help in sensitive positions. Family loyalty, one of the most basic supports any man can have, is in effect denied to men in public office. Such an attitude is morally indefensible. Moreover, it is basically hostile to Biblical faith, which stresses the centrality of the family in every aspect of life.

The Bible does *not* treat nepotism as a crime but rather as a moral necessity. If nepotism is a crime and a moral wrong, then we are condemning God, who in some cases specifically required or commanded it. It was God who called and ordained that Aaron, Moses' brother, should become Moses' closest associate. When Moses became the civil head of the Hebrew commonwealth, Aaron, by God's ordination, became the religious head, the high priest, and Miriam, his sister, became a prophetess. As long as Aaron and Miriam fulfilled their duties, God blessed them; when they disobeyed and presumed on their relationship, they were punished. King David relied very extensively on his family, and especially his cousins, such as Joab, in the government of Israel, and virtually every monarch in the Bible relied on relatives without anything but God's blessing, as long as all moved in terms of God's law. The Bible is clearly favorable to the use of relatives in civil administration, and it is clearly not morally permissible for a Christian to condemn the legitimate and useful employment of relatives.

Therefore, whenever and wherever nepotism is condemned, it is condemned on a moral principle which is not Biblical and is in fact anti-Biblical. The office of high priest, in the time of Jesus Christ, was passed around the family of Annas, the high priest, to his son, Eleazar and his son-in-law Caiaphas. The Biblical condemnation of these men is not because of their nepotism, but because of their unbelief. Two of the disciples, James and John, were cousins of Jesus Christ. The Bible, from start to finish, is strongly family oriented. Provided the members of a family are godly, there is no wrong in their employment and much good.

We face today an anti-Biblical morality which is at war with Biblical morality and therefore the family. It is called morally wrong to employ members of our family, but it is treated as somehow virtuous to trust our mortal enemies. Parents are told that it is wrong for them to assist their children in learning how to read, but they are urged to go into the slums and help other people's children. Parents are treated as moral lepers for being partial to their children above all others, and one prominent educator has called it an anti-democratic and aristocratic sentiment.[2] Somehow, it is insinuated that it is morally wrong to be partial to your own family. All this anti-family talk and sentiment goes against the law of God as declared in the Bible and in the laws of being.

These attacks on the family are part of a movement to replace a familistic order with another order, a statist one, to replace personal relations with impersonal ones. We have abolished, or are trying to abolish, the strongly personal feelings that generate family loyalties; we are treating family associations in business administration or in civil government as somehow immoral, and, by batteries of tests and requirements, we are depersonalizing offices and civil service. Supposedly, we

---

2. James Bryant Conant, *Education in a Divided World* (Cambridge, MA: Harvard University Press, 1948), 8.

are abolishing prejudice and discrimination. In actuality, we are *first*, establishing prejudice legally against the family. *Second*, by depersonalizing offices and the civil service, we are not furthering love but rather enmity. We abolish loyalty, and by abolishing loyalty, we diminish integrity and faithfulness.

It is high time we abandon the idea that any set of tests, laws, or rules can give us a perfect social order or a perfect group of employees or civil service. Nothing is more productive of social chaos than the attempt to create a perfect system. Men are by nature sinners; they can be saved sinners, but they will never in this world be perfect, sinless men. We need to live in terms of the realities of this world. We cannot gain progress by striving after an impossible perfection and destroying at the same time the God-given foundations of social order. The family is basic to God's order; it is man's basic social security and responsibility, the area of closest loyalty and strength. How dare we deny to public officials the right to rely on their most loyal supporters, their relatives, in their administration of office? Every man in office has a right to depend on his family, and to help them secure employment. Instead of being morally wrong, it is morally commendable, as long as honest work is rendered for honest wages. Is it not time we dropped this extensive hostility to the family?

TWENTY-SEVEN

THE FLIGHT FROM LIFE

One of the dominant aspects of modern life is *escapism.* Not only in literature, but in all the arts, there is a rebellion against the realities of life and a systematic attempt to find refuge in a dream world.

A prominent area of escape for the past century has been the academic world, the university in particular. Men who found the realities of the workaday world unpleasant turned to the university as a way out. It was not scholarship they loved, but the business world which they hated. To them the test of a working world was anathema; they were in a sense a new kind of hermit, running away from the civilized world and renouncing it for a new way of life. Speaking of some of these men in England, the critic, Edmund Wilson, spoke of them as belonging to the "monastic order of English university ascetics."[1] Their asceticism was forsaking the world of capitalism and Christianity, the world of the family and its morality, for a new order, an anti-Christian one. Everything in

---

1. Edmund Wilson, *Eight Essays* (Garden City, NY: Doubleday Anchor Books, 1954), 127.

the old world was and is to these men evil and anathema, and
they denounce it with religious intensity and passion.

The basic fallacy of these men was and is their flight from
reality. Now a rebellion against the injustices and evils of this
world is a healthy and necessary reaction in every generation.
Progress is in part a product of discontent, an unwillingness to
accept the status quo and a desire to establish better law and
order, greater justice, and a stronger sense of community.
Inventions have been a product of man's restlessness with
inadequate devices and a desire to improve on techniques and
devices. Progress, however, comes only when men move in
terms of a sense of reality, not in flight from reality. To cite a
commonplace illustration, two brothers from a particularly
underprivileged home both sought to escape it. One sought
refuge in liquor first and then later in narcotics; the other
studied at night until he was able to qualify for a responsible
and well-paying position.

But history has periodically seen men in full rebellion
against reality and in flight from it. They seek to conform life
and reality to their dream world, to impossibilities which seem
wonderful in imagination but produce horror and destruction
when forced onto reality. For a man of seventy-five to dream
of being twenty-one again is foolish enough, but to attempt to
play the part of a young man of twenty-one is insanity. It is a
flight from both reality and life, because life can be lived only
in terms of reality.

The university is still a major form of escapism. The perpetual student who is unwilling to grow up and leave the university is a common fact today. Most universities are crowded
with non-students or unweaned students who cling to the
school because they are unwilling to face the hated adult
world of work and responsibility.

Politics, however, has become an even more important
form of escapism. The political escapist hates reality, and he
plans to abolish reality by means of political action.

Basic to the Biblical faith is individual responsibility. Man is a sinner, accountable to God, redeemable only by Jesus Christ, and the focal point of social change must be the heart of man. But, because man is a sinner, he is unwilling to accept responsibility for his sin, nor is he ready to blame himself for his failures. Instead, his basic presupposition is that all is well with him and all is wrong with the world. Therefore, his every answer to his problems is to change the world, not himself.

For Karl Marx, this meant *revolution.* Marx had a religious belief in the power of revolution to create a paradise on earth. The result of the destruction of the old order would be the birth of a new order. This faith was plainly stated by the Marxists in Russia at the Second Congress of the Party, August 1903:

> By introducing social, instead of private, ownership of the means of production and exchange, by introducing well-regulated organization in the social process of production so that the well-being and the many-sided development of all members of society may be insured, the social revolution of the proletariat will abolish the division of society into classes and thus emancipate all oppressed humanity, and will put an end to all forms of exploitation of one part of society by another.[2]

It was actually believed that the revolution would abolish exploitation and class division; in actuality, it increased them. This 1903 Manifesto is one of the four great Communist manifestoes. Some of the things this manifesto called for are of interest. Thus, it called for "Local self-government on a wide scale; home rule for all localities where the population is of special composition and characterized by special conditions of life." It also demanded "Inviolability of person and dwelling. Unlimited freedom of religion, speech, press, assembly, strikes, and unions. Freedom of movement and occupation." Of course, the very opposite of this is the rule in all Marxist countries. But this is not all. The manifesto called for an

---

2. Thomas P. Whitney, ed., *The Communist Blueprint for the Future: The Complete Texts of All Four Communist Manifestos 1844–1961* (New York: Dutton, 1962), 68.

"Eight hour work day for all hired labor," and also for the "Complete prohibition of overtime work" and the "Prohibition of night work (from 9 P. M. to 6 A. M.) in all the branches of national economy, with the exception of those in which this is absolutely necessary because of technical considerations approved by labor organizations; Prohibition of the employment of children of school age ... Prohibition of women's labor in all branches of industry injurious to women's health." The manifesto cited "the need for a complete Socialist overturn, as the only way of abolishing all poverty and all exploitation."[3] The "necessary condition for this social revolution is the dictatorship of the proletariat."[4] The revolution, according to the manifesto, would bring about a translation from "barbarism ... the tsarist monarchy," to "a democratic republic whose constitution would guarantee" liberty.[5]

The reality, of course, is that the revolution which the Marxists of 1903 brought about in 1917 in Russia not only did not bring about the glorious new world they dreamed of but created a tyranny which executed virtually every surviving framer of the 1903 Manifesto. Instead of a glorious liberty, the result was a brutal reign of terror, one which continues to this day.

The root cause of the failure of the Marxist dream is that it represents a *flight from reality*. Marxism denies the Biblical doctrine of original sin. Instead of dealing realistically with man as sinner, it holds to the neutral or even good nature of man and his perfectibility. This means that, instead of distrusting man and hedging him in with checks and balances in the state, Marxism trusts power in the hands of men and creates a totalitarian state. The result of this inability to see man as he is, is an inability to live in terms of reality. The Marxist lacks the capacity to govern because he knows neither his own nature nor the nature of man everywhere. He lives under the illusion that his Marxist dream represents inevitable historical truth instead of error. As a result, his mental perspective is no

---

3. Ibid., 69–73.
4. Ibid., 68.
5. Ibid., 69.

different than that of the insane; he regards his illusions as reality and insists on living in terms of his illusions. As a consequence, his government can produce only chaos and destruction; it is a perpetual hindrance to the very productivity it demands of the people. The Marxist state accuses the people of sabotaging the national economy, when the actual saboteur is the Marxist state.

This flight from reality infects more than the Marxists of our time. It infects, as we have seen, the world of the university. It also infects liberalism, which builds also on the fallacious premise of the goodness of man. Some forms of political conservatism, because they reject Christian foundations, are guilty of the same illusion concerning man.

Every failure to recognize man as a sinner, every failure to face reality as it is before we begin to deal with it constructively, is not only a flight from reality but a flight from life. We are running away from life if we refuse to face it as it is, if we demand that life conform itself to our illusions.

Dostoyevsky saw clearly the implications of the radical thinkers of his day. Starting from unlimited freedom, they arrived at unlimited despotism. Mankind was divided into two unequal parts: "One-tenth is to enjoy absolute freedom and unbounded power over the other nine-tenths. The others must give up all individuality and become something like a herd to attain, through boundless submission and by a series of regenerations, a state of primeval innocence, something like the Garden of Eden." In effect, what the advocates of this socialist world demand is the right to become gods and rule over all other men. For men to imagine themselves to be gods is a flight from reality into monstrous delusions. Dostoyevsky has a radical declare, "Everyone belongs to all, and all belongs to everyone. All are slaves and equal in their slavery ... Slaves are bound to be equal. Without despotism there has never been either freedom or equality, but in the herd there is bound to be equality ... The moment you have family ties or love you have the desire for property. We will destroy that

desire. We shall reduce everything to a common denomi-
nator: complete equality, complete obedience, complete loss
of individuality."

Dostoyevsky attempted to warn man of what was coming,
but men failed to heed his warning, because they shared the
same humanistic illusions concerning man. They refused to
face the fact of man's total depravity; they were themselves
too guilty of the desire to be gods to see this urge as sin in
other men.

Basic to every flight from reality is a flight from creature-
hood, an unwillingness to accept the fact that we are men, not
gods. Satan's basic temptation, and man's original sin, is the
attempt to be as gods, knowing or determining good and evil
for ourselves (Gen. 3:5). Man was created by God to be a man,
not a god, and given a glorious destiny as man under God.
Man was summoned to be a king, priest, and prophet under
God over the earth, but man sinned by attempting to be his
own god. In Jesus Christ, man is restored to his destiny. Apart
from Jesus Christ, man lives under the illusion that his *sin*, to
be as god, is *fact*, and he attempts to make his word become
flesh, that is his illusion to become fact. The consequence is
destruction and chaos.

Every flight from reality is suicidal; it is a flight also from
life. Life can be realized in its potentialities only on God's
terms, not man's. Christ's words, speaking as Wisdom, are still
true: "He that sinneth against me wrongeth his own soul: all
they that hate me love death" (Prov. 8:36).

TWENTY-EIGHT

THE FLIGHT
FROM KNOWLEDGE

Oliver Wendell Holmes, Jr., was not only the leading American champion of legal positivism, but he was also prominent in the relativistic hostility to knowledge. In a letter to Harold Laski, dated October 30, 1930, Holmes observed, "I detest a man who knows that he knows." In part, Holmes's remark had reference to fanatics who manifested an irrational insistence on the truth of their position, but Holmes had more in mind than this. Basically, his position was the same as that of a later chief justice, Frederick Moore Vinson, who said, "Nothing is more certain in modern society than the principle that there are no absolutes." Vinson and Holmes were both relativists; for them there was no truth, no absolute right or wrong. Their perspective was pragmatic and positivistic, and, of course, anti-Christian.

The possibility of true knowledge concerning ultimate reality is denied by relativism. It is held that man cannot know God, if He exists, nor can he know the world of nature truly. He can *use* reality, but he cannot truly *know* it.

Not only this, but the attempt to gain knowledge is itself condemned. According to Comte, the father of sociology, the quest for meaning and knowledge represents the theological and metaphysical stages of history. Now, in the scientific stage, man moves not in terms of myth and meaning, not in terms of knowledge, but in terms of utility. The real question, we are told, is not "What does this mean?" but, "How can I use it?" Man must renounce meaning and knowledge for the pragmatic use of things. *The goal of learning therefore is not knowledge but the power to manipulate.* In dealing with either men or things, our purpose under pragmatism and relativism becomes not a knowledge of them but the power to manipulate them.

Education today is under the influence of this relativistic philosophy and expressive of it. Whether in its Marxist, existentialist, pragmatic, instrumentalist, progressivistic, or other forms, modern education is hostile to knowledge and in flight from knowledge. Its negative function is to indoctrinate its subjects with a radical cynicism concerning the family, patriotism, religion, philosophy, theology, and all things else. The student must be divorced from meaning and knowledge and married to power, because, it is held, knowledge is power.

As a result, all the traditional subjects have been changed. History is no longer treated as history, the knowledge of the past; it is social science now, the science of human control, and, when the past is studied, it is in terms of controlling the present. Philosophy too has changed; it is no longer, as its name indicates, the love of wisdom or knowledge. Its basic disciplines, epistemology and metaphysics, are treated with contempt. Philosophy has become a tool of power. It is instrumental to science and social controls. The idea that true knowledge should be the goal of philosophy is ridiculed as pre-scientific expectation. Philosophy too is in full-scale retreat from knowledge.

Much of philosophy has become logical analysis, the study of words and their use as instruments of power. Semantics too is interested in language only in the instrumental sense. Thus,

S. I. Hayakawa has observed, "Identification is something that goes on in the human nervous system. 'Out there' there are no absolute identities."[1] In other words, there is no truth, and therefore man is free to pioneer in this world without any restrictions or inhibitions.

Education today is therefore concerned, not with knowledge in its true sense, in its historic meaning, but with *the techniques of power.* We call it technical education or technical knowledge, but it is simply the ability to use the techniques of a profession, not the knowledge of things. It becomes increasingly difficult in every sphere to speak in terms of knowledge: people are interested in power. Even in the churches, this basic pragmatism prevails. It is not knowledge of God and His word that men seek, but rather how to live more successfully, how to find peace, how to win friends, and the like. The basic question asked of religion is this, "What is God doing for man?" People go to church not to worship, not to submit themselves to God and to gain knowledge from God's word, but to advance themselves psychologically and socially. And increasingly it is held that the church is not truly the church unless it works to further the social revolution. The church itself has become another pragmatic tool of humanistic man.

The flight from knowledge means basically an anti-social movement. To deny that there is any absolute truth and absolute knowledge is to deny that there is a God who is the center and lord over all things, and whose order and truth governs and is the source of all truth and knowledge. If there is no absolute knowledge in God and from God in His revelation, then the only absolute in any man's life is himself. Every man is his own god, his own law, and his own source of knowledge. His self-knowledge is the only knowledge possible to him, because there is then no other truth than man. Man's purpose becomes power over other men, that control over the world of men and things which will prove to himself that he is the god

---

1. S. I. Hayakawa, "How Words Change Our Lives," *Saturday Evening Post,* December 27, 1958.

which he believes he is. As a result, he isolates himself from all men, withdraws into the solitariness of his imagined godhood. And, together with all the other men who delude themselves with the same pretensions of godhood, he becomes a member of the "lonely crowd." Instead of being a man among men, he sees himself as a god among men, and his goal becomes, not to love or hate men, that is, to have *personal* relationships with them, but to use men, to *manipulate* them impersonally. As a result, in the name of humanity, this man-god treats mankind as an object to be used and manipulated.

The modern humanist is in secession from society. He is in flight from knowledge and in full-scale retreat from reality. The humanist is compelled to deny the possibility of knowledge, because it is the only possible way he can imagine of denying God. David declared, "The heavens declare the glory of God; and the firmament sheweth his handywork. Day unto day uttereth speech, and night unto night sheweth knowledge. There is no speech nor language, where their voice is not heard" (Ps. 19:1–3). As St. Paul said, "that which may be known of God is manifest in them; for God hath shewed it unto them. For the invisible things of him from the creation of the world are clearly seen, being understood by the things that are made, even his eternal power and Godhead; so that they are without excuse" (Rom. 1:19–20). All man's knowledge witnesses to God, and the law and order of God's creation witnesses to God, so that man faces everywhere the inescapable knowledge of God. The knowledge of God is inescapable, because all things were created by God and therefore witness to Him. Every fact is a God-created fact and therefore can only witness to God.There are no brute facts in the universe, only God-created and God-ordained facts. Every fact therefore proclaims God when it is truly known.

The only way the humanist believes that he can escape God is to deny the possibility of knowledge. The purpose of relativism in its every form is to shut the door in the face of God, to deny the possibility of all knowledge, because all knowledge testifies to God. It is not merely the *denial* of knowledge but the intense *flight* from knowledge which characterizes relativism. Relativism is the modern form of atheism. It is far more radical that the older atheism, which merely denied God; relativism denies not only God but all knowledge.

Relativism therefore unleashes the forces of total negation. It creates a hostility on all fronts to all law and order, to every institution except the power state. It attacks the family, because it hates the ties of family love. Family love involves subordination to an accepted law and order, to parents, to the responsibility of being a husband or a wife. Such subordination and responsibility is intolerable to these humanistic gods. The only relationship tolerable to them is "free love," that is, a relationship without obligation or responsibility, a relationship which can be assumed freely or dropped just as freely. It is an intolerable concept for these humanistic gods to be chained to domestic responsibilities.

Total negation means total hatred. As a result, relativism attacks every kind of loyalty, faith, and responsibility. Love involves affirmation; love means loyalty and association; it means responsibility. For men to maintain the illusion that they are the gods of creation, it is important for them to maintain their independence from all other men and from all ties and responsibilities. As a result, humanism leads to man's isolation from man, to man's hatred of every tie that binds him, every love that claims him. Total negation is total hatred.

Total negation is also total ignorance. The flight from knowledge can culminate, logically, only in ignorance, because relativism and pragmatism are dedicated to a systematic ignorance of certain knowledge. It is not surprising therefore that progressive education produces academic ignorance, nor that existentialism breeds an unwashed, boorish, and ignorant herd of followers.

The flight from knowledge, however, is doomed to frustration. Since man also is a God-created fact, man can nowhere escape the knowledge of God, neither in the world nor in the

recesses of his being. David made clear this inescapable knowledge of God in Psalm 139:7–12:

> Whither shall I go from thy spirit? Or whither shall I flee
> from thy presence?
> If I ascend up into heaven, thou art there: if I make my bed
> in hell, behold, thou art there.
> If I take the wings of the morning, and dwell in the utter-
> most parts of the sea;
> Even there shall thy hand lead me, and thy right hand shall
> hold me.
> If I say, Surely the darkness shall cover me; even the night
> shall be light about me.
> Yea, the darkness hideth not from thee; but the night
> shineth as the day: the darkness and the light are both
> alike to thee.

Men can escape neither from God nor from the knowledge of
God. St. Paul declared that, in the fullness of time, "every knee
should bow, of things in heaven, and things in earth, and
things under the earth; And that every tongue should confess
that Jesus Christ is Lord, to the glory of God the Father" (Phil.
2:10–11). The inescapable knowledge of God shall bring inescapable submission to Jesus Christ, either as Savior or as
Judge.

The conclusion of the flight from knowledge is the grim
reality of the inescapable knowledge of judgment. Every individual and every civilization is faced with the fact of inescapable knowledge. Either they dedicate themselves to the
knowledge of God and the knowledge of all things in Him, or
they face the inescapable knowledge of God in the form of
judgment.

TWENTY-NINE

SOCIALISM AS A
PERPETUAL CIVIL WAR

Socialism and communism presuppose that their system represents the true order of the ages and is the answer to man's problems. This assumption is one that assumes man's problems to be not spiritual but material, not sin but environment. Change man's environment and you will then remake man, it is held. The answer to man's problems is therefore not the spiritual regeneration of man by Jesus Christ but the reorganization of society by the *scientific* socialist state.

Basic to the theory of scientific socialism is its infallibility concept. Every system of thought has an infallibility concept, but few are honest enough to admit it. Ultimate, final, and inerrant authority is vested somewhere in the system as the basic and assured arbiter of truth or reality. The *scientific* socialistic state sees scientific socialism as the infallible truth of history; its application ensures the perfect social order. If failures occur in scientific socialist states, it is not the fault of scientific socialism, which is by definition infallible and true, but of the hostile people, remnants of the capitalistic class, or traitorous members of the party. Because the scientific socialist state cannot blame itself, it must wage civil war against some portion of the state. Thus, *first* of all, socialism's answer to every problem is civil war. Someone is guilty, but never socialism itself.

Illustrations of this are many. The Soviet Union has faced a situation of continual purges. The purges of the 1930s stand out merely as being more dramatic than the routine ones. But every crisis in the Soviet Union demands a scapegoat, and war is therefore waged against some portion of the Party, the bureaucracy, or the masses.

In Communist China, according to a news report of Friday, March 24, 1967, pestilence broke out widely, with many contagious diseases spreading across the country. The Communist regime's answer to an already serious crisis was to threaten the doctors of China with a purge. The doctors were responsible, the Shanghai Radio declared, because they "had ignored Mao's health policies."[1] The consequence of such a policy, the purge of doctors in a country with a serious shortage of medical men, only aggravated a serious situation, but anything is preferable to admitting that socialism can make mistakes and be an erroneous theory.

In the United States, inflation is a product of the federal government's departure from a hard money standard, from gold to paper, and a product of its debt living or deficit financing. The guilt for inflation is essentially the federal government's guilt. But the blame is instead shifted by federal officials to the private sector: labor is creating inflation by demanding higher wages, and business is inflationary because it demands higher prices for goods, and threats are made of wage and price controls. The demands of capital and labor are, of course, the *results* of inflation and their steps to protect themselves against it, but the policy of socialism is to ascribe all guilt to the people, and all wisdom to the state, in every crisis.

---

1. Oakland *Tribune*, "China Hit by Outbreak of Pestilence," Friday, March 24, 1967, 1.

In these and other cases, the answer always remains the same: the socialist state wages war on the people. Whenever the scientific socialist state makes a mistake, the people suffer.

The *second* aspect of this socialist civil warfare is that it is perpetual civil war because of perpetual failure. Socialism is incapable of solving any problem it addresses itself to in the economic sphere. Because its premises are unsound and wholly in error, its conclusions are consistently failures. But, since socialism is by definition the *scientific* answer to problems of society, socialism cannot blame itself. As a result, it wages perpetual civil warfare as its answer to perpetual failure.

Third, the consequence of this perpetual civil warfare is an ever-deepening crisis. Propaganda works to disguise the crisis. We are always told that the Soviet Union is making economic and industrial progress and is becoming a milder dictatorship, but the reality is that it has merely gone from crisis to crisis and has faced a growing food shortage as a tribute to its incompetence. The other socialisms of the world have similar troubles. The little Fabian Socialist State of Great Britain is sinking steadily into the economic consequences of its own policies, and other Fabian states face a growing monetary and economic crisis. Socialism is never the way out for socialism, but simply the guarantee of an economic dead end.

Fourth, this perpetual civil warfare can and will terminate in the death of the state, and possibly of the civilization as well. It is destructive of the public and private resources of the state; the socialist state can sometimes build stone monuments and edifices, but it cannot perpetuate a living social order; it can only kill the order it seizes or inherits. It has often been observed that it is only when a civilization is dying that it begins monumental building constructions. Prior to that time, its concern is more with life than show. We cannot therefore misread socialism's predisposition for monumental construction as a sign of life; it is tombstone construction.

Fifth, perpetual civil warfare means in some form perpetual violence or repressive force, and as a result, the use of terror is not only accepted but is often justified and exalted. Terror is defended and upheld as necessary to suppress the enemies of the people and to protect the state from destruction. Jean-Paul Sartre, in his *Critique of Dialectical Reason,* spoke of terror as "the very bond of fraternity." Terror is made a moral principle and an inevitable requirement of history. As a result, "total terror" is practiced as a necessary and moral requirement of scientific socialism. Incredible brutality, barbarism, savagery, and degeneracy become the products of scientific socialism.[2] Thus, the perpetual civil warfare that the scientific socialist state wages against its people is also a form of *total warfare.* It is more radical than total warfare, in that normal total warfare is for a stated period of hostilities, whereas the socialistic civil war and its terroristic total warfare have no end. It is a perpetual threat to the people, and, in varying degrees, continuously practiced. The more the state approaches total socialism, to that same degree it also approaches total terror and total civil war. It is this aspect of perpetual and total warfare that has made socialists like George Orwell, author of *1984,* turn from socialism in horror, without believing really in anything else. Theirs is not a conversion but simply revulsion from terror.

Such a situation, of course, breaks down the will to work and the will to live of the subject peoples. Hope of escape, or hope that the socialist regime will end, begins to grow weaker, and the result is all the greater slow-down in agricultural and industrial production. This decline in productivity creates a major crisis, and the socialist leaders must give the people some reason to believe that there is hope of a change, a "thaw," in the socialist terror and oppression. A cow, after all, will finally give no milk if it is not fed, and so the masses, like human cattle, are given enough fodder to make them productive again. Their previous sufferings are blamed on bad underlings, poor managers. Stalin, for example, placed the blame

---

2. See Albert Kalme, *Total Terror: an Expose of Genocide in the Baltics* (New York: Appleton-Century-Crofts, 1951); and Harold H. Martinson, *Red Dragon Over China* (Minneapolis: Augsburg, 1956).

on minor officials who were supposedly too eager to attain perfect socialism overnight. In dealing with enforced collectivization of farms, in a *Pravda* statement of April 3, 1930, Stalin declared that the policy was a "voluntary one," but unfortunately some officials were using threats and pressure.[3] It was *after* this statement that millions were starved to death for resisting collectivization, but Stalin in advance had cleared himself publicly of responsibility and also encouraged those who were hostile to feel freer to make a stand. Khrushchev also gave promises of a thaw, and then launched into the vicious terror in Hungary, and the still-continuing and greatest terror against Christians.

The purposes of these brief thaws and breathers are strategic: they serve to give a despairing populace hope for a change. This, then, is simply a *sixth*, aspect of socialism's civil warfare against its people. The thaw creates a deviation from socialist policy only for the purpose of reinforcing that policy.

This points clearly to a *seventh* aspect of socialism's perpetual civil war: truth is at all times a central casualty. Since there is no truth apart from the scientific socialist state, any device, any lie, any strategy which will further the socialist experiment is valid. The lie is spoken to delude the masses and the enemy; speech has as its purpose not the communication of truth but utility to the dictatorship of the proletariat as a weapon of warfare. Semantics therefore becomes a major concern of socialism. Language must be used; it is a superb weapon. Certain words have powerful meanings to many men, and one way of using men's minds against themselves is to misuse the words that have a particular meaning to them. To expect language to have the same content to a socialist as it does to a Christian is a delusion. For the socialist, language is instrumental; it is a tool of revolution. Instead of representing a means of communicating an objective order of truth, language is basically an instrument of power. For the socialist

---

3. W. R. Werner, ed., *Stalin Kampf: Joseph Stalin's Credo, Written by Himself* (New York: Howell, Soskin and Company, 1940), 252–257.

state to neglect to use language as an instrument of power is for it to be guilty of bourgeois sentiments and illusions.

This, then, is the course of action, perpetual civil warfare, required by the scientific socialist state to maintain its delusion of infallibility. This perpetual civil warfare is a consequence of its departure from God and its socialism. It is a suicidal course, one well described by our Lord of old, when He declared, "He that sinneth against me wrongeth his own soul: all they that hate me love death" (Prov. 8:36).

THIRTY

POLITICS AND EDUCATION

During the early 1967 Berkeley student demonstrations against the possibility of a tuition fee, an excellent phrase was coined by some of the demonstrators: *Keep politics out of education.* It is high time we gave this principle serious thought. We need to keep politics out of education. The state has no more business running the schools than it has running the churches, and it has no more ground for financing education than it has for financing churches. What is needed badly is the disestablishment of the schools—the separation of school and state.

Education is not the function of the state; it is the function of educators. A lawyer, barber, minister, oil geologist, or cattleman—all operate without benefit of any subsidy from any branch of civil government. They survive because, first, their services are needed, and, second, their services are better than those of their competitors. A subsidy destroys quality; it keeps the failures in a field of activity from paying the price of failure, from going out of business. Because a subsidy enables a failure to keep going, it keeps incompetence alive and makes it at least equal to competence.

Certainly, education is necessary to society, but churches are also very necessary, as are doctors, lawyers, mechanics, and most professions and trades. Does necessity entitle them to a subsidy? A subsidy is a form of establishment; it is also a form of capture. Whenever and wherever a civil government finances any kind of activity, it has the legal and moral right to control that activity. If the state finances the churches, it has a right to control the churches. If the state finances the schools, colleges, and universities, it has a right and a duty to control them.

Some will object, however, that not everyone then could afford an education. The answer is that before state support of education began in the United States, all American children were educated. The children of the poor and of immigrants were educated by educational missionary societies. Moreover, it is a mistake to think that we do not pay for education when it is state supported. We not only pay for it, but we pay more. Recently, two schools were built in one community, for about an equal number of children, but the Christian school cost only half as much as the state school and gives a better education. It must be added too that the educational tax burden on the poor man is very much heavier than any Christian school tuition; he pays that tax directly or indirectly, almost every time he turns around.

State supported education is totalitarian education. The essence of totalitarianism is simply this, that it maintains that the state has all the answers to life, and virtually every sphere of human activity should be governed by the state. The totalitarian believes that education, economics and trade, the family, child welfare, old age welfare, medicine, science, and all things else need the controlling and guiding hand of the state. There are different kinds of totalitarianism—Marxist, democratic, Fascist, Fabian, and the like—but their differences are not basic, whereas their agreements are. Common to all forms of totalitarianism is a belief in the state control of education. From Plato's blueprint for a communist state to the present, totalitarian planning has counted heavily on the control of education.

Christian libertarianism is hostile to politics in education. It is also not in favor of the church in education. The school is as free an agency under God as are church and state. Neither church nor state has any right to control the other, or any right to control the family, economics, farming, art, or any other sphere of human activity. No institution has the right to play god and guardian over all other institutions in society. For any institution to claim this right is totalitarian. The family does not belong to either the church or the state; it is a separate institution under God directly. The school similarly has a right to a free and separate existence. It is an independent realm, with a markedly different function than that of either church or state.

The function of the school and of the teacher is to teach, to educate. If the state or the church controls the school then it becomes the function of the school to serve the purposes of the state or of the church. Propaganda begins to govern education. Instead of serving the primary function of the school or college, the teacher then serves the primary purpose of the controlling state or church. Moreover, the quality of the school declines, because the school then exists by means of a subsidy from another institution, not because it is doing a successful job.

A truly successful school is one whose purposes and teachings so greatly please a certain group of people that they voluntarily support it, pay their tuition fees to enter it, and feel its existence is important enough to promote it.

Under the system of free schools—unsubsidized schools— some schools will teach in terms of a Christian faith, others in terms of humanism, but each school will depend on its merits and on popular support to keep it going. This is exactly how the churches survive, and we are not underchurched. This is also how business survives, by meeting the public demand with a superior product that sells readily.

Non-statist education today is American's fastest growing social movement. Every year more and more Christian and private schools are being established, and many have long waiting lists. These schools do not represent the wealthier classes only. One of the finest schools I have visited was established in a small town, and most of the children are from mill-working families, almost all of very modest incomes. These schools are being established because parents are demanding an education that meets their requirements, not the state's. Today between twenty-five and thirty percent of all grade school children are not in public schools; they are in private, parochial, and Christian day schools. Ten percent of all U. S. high school students are also in non-statist schools. The percentage is increasing rapidly. This is the major social revolution of our day, and yet the newspapers rarely mention it. Since 1950, the education scene has seen a major shift away from statist education on the grade and high school levels, but few are aware of this revolutionary fact. At the present rate of growth, by the end of this century, the public school will be gone and the independent school will have replaced it.

The slogan, *Keep politics out of education*, is both a good and a necessary one. Education needs freedom to survive. The academic world has too long been a refuge for misfits who thrive in a subsidized world. The average professor today is not a scholar. He is ready to do research only as long as it is necessary for promotion. Once he becomes a full professor and has tenure, he becomes disinterested in learning, because his world is a better hiding place *from* education than a place *for* education. Few professors are adequate teachers; they are not enough interested in either teaching or scholarship to do more than go through the motions. Karl Jaspers, an existentialist philosopher and a university professor, has admitted that the modern university is basically anti-intellectual and hostile to excellence. Because it is the refuge of mediocre men, Jaspers said, "The excellent are instinctively excluded from fear of competition."[1]

---

1. Karl Jaspers, *The Idea of the University*, 71.

In the sciences, although untold millions are poured annually into the graduate schools and research facilities of our universities, the results are very poor. The basic advances in research come from private laboratories, from men who must produce in terms of the market. Science advances best, not under subsidy, but under competition and the necessity to provide in terms of profits.

Subsidized education is productive, not in terms of the needs of the world at large, but in terms of the demands of politicians. The school is geared to the needs of the state, not in terms of a working world. The result is a growing incompetence in public education. The more education develops in terms of its state-oriented purposes, the more incompetent it becomes. When politics governs education, it is politics that is the gainer, and education which becomes the loser. Education has declined steadily as the political control over it has increased. Thus, the *National Fifth Reader* from the 1850s was so far ahead of the *McGuffy Fifth Reader* that there is no comparison, and now we have many who look back to *McGuffy* as superior to the present readers. The decline is real, because the school is geared to politics rather than education, and the decline will only increase more rapidly in the next few years.

The independent schools are rapidly gaining ground because they offer superior education. Instead of improving the caliber of the education they offer, some statist educators have instead expressed the opinion that independent schools should be either outlawed or taken over by the state. This is the totalitarian answer to problems: outlaw the competition. In 1925, in the Oregon Case, the U. S. Supreme Court ruled, "The fundamental theory of liberty upon which all governments in the Union repose excludes any general power of the state to standardize its children by forcing them to accept instruction from public teachers only;" in other words, independent education is basic to American liberty. But John L. Childs, professor emeritus of Columbia Teachers College, questioned this right a few years ago, stating, "Unless church

educational practices which are assumed to have been sanc-
tioned by that historic decision of the Supreme Court are
reviewed and revised, the future of the common school is not
one of promise." Against this attitude, we must firmly insist:
Take politics out of education; let us stand for separation of state
and school.

THIRTY-ONE

PLANNING FOR FAMINE

A distinguished American, E. Parmalee Prentice, who wrote two important works on the subject of famine, *Farming for Famine*, written in 1936, and *Hunger and History* in 1939, gives us a vivid picture of the fearful role of famine in man's life. On page after page, he recounts the centuries-old horror of death by starvation, of people eating the bark of trees, resorting to cannibalism and the eating of their own children, and still dying by the tens of thousands and even millions. This was common for ages and well into the eighteenth century.

The world at that time was sparsely populated. There was no shortage of land and growing space, but people lived meagerly most of the time. Hunger stalked every continent, and famine was commonplace. During one century alone, Prentice listed fifteen famines in England, and other famines in Scotland and Ireland. These famines in England were accompanied by the usual horrors: people eating the bark of trees, grass, turning to cannibalism, and dying on all sides. During the reign of Edward I, a twenty-three-year dearth saw the churches without any wine for communion.

In China, throughout the centuries, famine has been a part of the life of the people, and a normal part of the mortality rate. In Europe, before the beginning of the nineteenth century, the same thing was true: famine was a major cause of death and a normal part of life.

The one part of the world that has not known famine has been the United States. After the early years of colonization, America has seen, instead of hunger and famine, an abundance of food and a standard of eating unknown by royalty of ancient times. One of the vivid descriptions of farm life comes from *The Autobiography of Mark Twain*. In writing of his boyhood, Mark Twain said:

> It was a heavenly place for a boy, that farm of my Uncle John's. The house was a double log one, with a spacious floor (roofed in) connecting it with the kitchen. In the summer the table was set in the middle of that shady and breezy floor, and the sumptuous meals—well, it makes me cry to think of them. Fried chicken, roast pig; wild and tame turkeys, ducks and geese; venison just killed; squirrels, rabbits, pheasants, partridges, prairie chickens; biscuits, hot batter cakes, hot buckwheat cakes, succotash, butter-beans, string-beans, tomatoes, peas, Irish potatoes, sweet potatoes; butter-milk, sweet milk, "clabber"; watermelons, musk-melons, cantaloupes—all fresh from the garden; apple pie, peach pie, pumpkin pie, apple dumplings, peach cobbler—I can't remember the rest. The way that the things were cooked was perhaps the main splendor ..."

Before we dismiss Mark Twain's picture by saying that America was then young, rich, and underpopulated, let us remember that before the white man settled America, the Indians, who were perhaps at most 300,000 persons across the continent, starved regularly. Famine was a normal part of Indian life, and the reason was not overpopulation. In fact, this myth of overpopulation has nothing to do with the subject of food and the supply of food. People have, age after age, starved to death in lands with small populations and rich soil, and also lived richly in heavily populated areas.

Both Prentice and Cornelius Walford have pointed out that the basic causes for famine are not those we usually consider, but rather "human folly and ignorance." Storms and droughts are a normal part of human existence; nature is a condition of life, and man can protect himself to a considerable degree from natural disasters. Moreover, natural disasters tend to be local, confined to a particular area. It does not flood everywhere, but in a particular area. A cyclone strikes a particular region, not a whole nation. The basic causes of famine are man-made, and man's greatest problem is to protect himself against himself. Now according to Walford and Prentice, four important causes of famine are the following:

1. The prevention of cultivation or the willful destruction of crops;
2. Defective agriculture caused by communistic control of land;
3. Governmental interference by regulation or taxation;
4. Currency restrictions, including debasing the coin.

These four factors add up to one thing, *socialism.* A major product of socialism is always agricultural chaos and famine. The old Russia was the breadbasket of Europe. It has had several major famines and a chronic agricultural problem since going communist.

The United States, in Mark Twain's day, was a free country, and its production of food was the envy of the world. Much of the world has rich soil, but little of the world has the free men to make use of that soil. Today, the United States is moving steadily into socialism, and into problems of food shortage. We have been stockpiling American-produced foods to give away, while importing the same foods often from abroad. The United States is now the world's second largest importer of farm commodities, second only to Great Britain. The very items that the federal government claims we are overproducing, we are at the same time importing, because we are short of them. Controls are leading us into economic chaos, and some of the very same federal officials are beginning to talk of the possibilities of food shortages and famine.

In the last century, when Europe joined America in freeing its economics of state controls, Europe, like America, enjoyed a famine-free century although its population in some areas more than doubled. Together, Europe and the United States set a standard of liberty, and economic security in freedom, for all the world, and all the continents began to experience a measure of victory over the ancient curse of famine. All over the world, with the growth of liberty populations increased, and the supply of food increased. It was free farmers who made possible a new growth of human welfare.

However, with the twentieth century, socialism offered a supposed short cut to paradise on earth—statist controls. As the tide turned towards socialism, so also did famine begin to return. The more severe the socialism, the more severe the famine. Instead of blaming socialism for hunger and famine, the socialists began to make excuses. Overpopulation is a myth created by these statists to excuse their growing failure to feed people. But the American Indians, as we have seen, starved regularly before the coming of the white man. Very commonly, they turned to cannibalism, and the very word cannibalism comes from the name of the Carib Indians of Haiti, whom Columbus met. The cannibalism of the Caribbeans was spoken of as a Caribbean practice, and the word Caribbean gradually changed to cannibal. The Indian tribes lacked freedom; tribalism in its various forms was a kind of primitive communism. Even the freest tribes, where private property had some standing, lacked the freedom that is necessary for initiative. As a result, the Indians starved regularly on a rich continent.

But the white settlers overpopulated America, as compared to the Indian population, and lived in plenty. The difference was liberty, faith, and hard work. By the sweat of their brow, the settlers made the land productive and rich. They made the name of America synonymous with liberty and wealth in the minds of all the peoples of the earth.

Now, however, we are supposedly going to overcome all man's problems by laws, regulations, and push buttons. In fact, former Secretary of Agriculture Orville L. Freeman has predicted that we will have "Farming by Satellite." By the year 2000, space satellites will give farmers the basic information for farming. According to Freeman, "While the farmers of tomorrow study reports in their air-conditioned offices, relieved at last of the physical drudgery and occupational anxiety so traditionally theirs, and the Secretary of Agriculture takes unaccustomed ease at his desk in Washington, these shining satellites, equipped with the most sophisticated remote sensing instruments, are supplying the information needed to make key decisions." Freeman went on to tell a convention of the National Association of Science Teachers, "Information gathered from throughout the world will be transmitted to computers for analysis and immediate use. The soils of the world will have been inventoried, and each crop will be grown either on the soil best suited for it, or on soil chemically modified for maximum productivity ... Through information gathered by the satellites, the government will be able to make accurate predictions to guide marketing and distribution of farm products to avoid waste and local shortages, and surpluses."[1] What Freeman is in effect saying is that the federal government, using the satellites, will analyze, control, and determine all farming in terms of an overall plan. This is, of course, not freedom: it is socialism. And it is planning for famine, because nothing will produce agricultural chaos more quickly than this central planning. Famine has long been a stranger to America. Not since the earliest settlement has it been felt on these shores. But hunger may again enter our history soon, if we continue our planning for famine.

---

1. "Coming Up—Farming By Satellite," in Oakland, California, *Tribune*, Monday, March 20, 1967, ES9.

THIRTY-TWO

THE WILL TO DEATH

In a book I have written, *Freud*, I have analyzed the theories of the founder of psychoanalysis and expressed my radical disagreement with them. At one point, Sigmund Freud did say something with which it is possible for us to agree. Freud spoke of two basic motive forces in man—the will to death and the will to live. Of these two, he felt the stronger and more basic force is the will to death, a suicidal drive to end life which governs the unconscious of men. Albert William Levi, in commenting on Freud, concluded, "We are thus compelled to say that the goal of all life is death." [1]

Our agreement with this is, of course, a limited one. For a Christian, since Jesus Christ is the new way of life within him, his basic drive is to live, to live righteously under God. The more he grows in grace, the more strongly will his will to live flourish. The strong Christian will be governed not only by a will to live but a will to victory. The psalmist declared, "I shall not die, but live, and declare the works of the LORD"

---

1. Albert William Levi, *Philosophy and the Modern World*, 165.

189

(Ps. 118:17). St. John declared that "this is the victory that overcometh the world, even our faith" (1 John 5:4).

When men are without faith, they are governed instead by an overpowering although unconscious will to death. In a study which, while defective at points from a Christian perspective is still very important, the psychologist Samuel J. Warner studies *The Urge to Mass Destruction*. In this urge to mass destruction, the individual will to death seeks to involve all men in its suicidal course. Warner cites "two major dynamic factors" which enter in the causation of this urge to mass destruction: *first*, "the craving for individual power," for the sheer amoral assertion of the ego, and *second*, "the motive of revenge." In this will to power, relativism and nihilism are basic. In answer to the question, "What does the nihilist believe?" Nietzsche wrote, in *The Will to Power*, "Nihilism is ... the belief that everything deserves to perish." Moreover, Nietzsche declared, "Thorough Nihilism is the conviction that life is absurd in the light of the highest values already discovered," and "the deed of Nihilism ... is suicide." We should not be surprised that today's radicals, with their relativism and nihilism, are demanding that, as individuals and a nation, we follow a course of deliberate suicide. Since they themselves are governed by a will to death, it is for them the only logical course of action.

Warner speaks of the necessity of understanding the "most malignant perversion of human mindedness. We proceed with a conception of human mindedness in which *hatred of all who live* is a key underlying feeling, *individual power* is a salient craving, and *revenge upon all who live* is a major factor." In other words, these zombies, these living dead, hate the living with all the passion of their malignant and corrupt souls. They dedicate their lives to the destruction of all life and want all things to perish.

For a man governed by the will to death, says Warner, it is "more important for him to defeat others than to succeed." Such a person is envious of success in others, hates them for it, but is both afraid of success and avoids it; he wills defeat and failure. He finds pleasure in unhappiness and misery, in defeat and in anxiety. In fact, states Warner, "*Victory through defeat* may indeed become the safest form of victory." Such a person consciously may be working for victory, but unconsciously aim for and welcome defeat. As a result, because so many millions all over the world are involved in this will to death, we have therefore a national and international mental condition which is best described by Warner's title, *The Urge to Mass Destruction.* We have now what Warner calls "the efforts of man to organize mass self-destruction … to seek a mass grave for all." He recognizes that hatred for the God of Scripture is basic to this will to death. The hatred of God, we can add, governs all men who are outside of Christ. Because their basic sin is the attempt to become a god, to determine or know good and evil independently of God, men find God a major obstacle in their drive for independence. As a result, they will the death of God, and in their diseased minds, imagine that He is abolished and dead. But, since man is a creature of God, man cannot wish the death of God, the ground of man's own existence, without thereby willing his own death. All atheism therefore is involved in this will to death.

The answers Warner gives to this problem of the urge to mass destruction are non-Christian and therefore fallacious, although his analysis is excellent and a major contribution.

We have this urge to mass destruction on all sides of us. It governs men in their political life, as we chart a suicidal course with reference to foreign affairs. We have it in our personal lives, and many men, as they sit behind the driver's wheel, seem very openly suicidal. We have the will to death present in rebellious youth, who deliberately experiment with death in the form of lawlessness and drugs and call their blindness, "living." We have this will to death in education, whereby proven values are forsaken for courses bound to increase ignorance and folly, and we have it in family life, as loose and careless exercise of authority by parents dissolves the life of the family.

The suicide rate, moreover, is increasing rapidly, and far more rapidly than statistics indicate. In almost all communities, only the most obvious cases are listed as suicide. To avoid public disgrace or religious problems for the family, the usual report conceals the fact of suicide.

But today suicide is the number two cause of death among college students, and the number three cause of death among those aged fifteen to nineteen years.[2] The reasons given by suicidal persons in their notes are of particular interest: they are uniformly trivial. Old and young routinely kill themselves for the most insignificant and trifling reasons.

It is obvious from this that their recorded reasons are not their real reasons. Because they are sinners, they are guilt-ridden, and guilt-ridden people are driven by a will to death. As a result, almost any pretext will do to drive them to suicide, because they are already driven there continually from within.

But those who do not openly and obviously commit suicide are no less driven by the will to death. They demand courses of action, personally and nationally, which can lead only to mass destruction, to mass suicide. They are dominated by a passion to involve others and the world itself in their headlong plunge to destruction.

They demand death in every area as their true morality. They favor a course of political and military suicide. They are for moral, spiritual, economic, and military disarmament as their quick way to death.

This urge to mass destruction is also present in the demand for abortion. It is significant that the eras in history which have favored abortion have also been the great ages for a high suicide rate. The two go hand in hand. They both represent a hatred of life. Joshua Lederberg, professor of genetics at Stanford, has said, in favoring abortion, "We cannot insist on absolute rights to life of a piece of tissue just because it bears a resemblance to humanity." The next step, of course,

---

2. Bernard Gavzer, "Suicide Increases Among Young," Oakland, California, *Tribune*, Wednesday, November 9, 1966, 24-A.

will be to deny anyone's right to life. If science has the right to take prenatal life, it has the right to take postnatal life, because it has become judge over life.

Not only do suicide and abortion go together, but the same people who demand the right of abortion, the right to kill prenatal life, claim also to be against capital punishment. This is not surprising; since they advocate murder by abortion, why punish postnatal murders by capital punishment? Their claim is that they favor life, but in reality, they demand freedom for the will to death.

Jesus Christ, speaking as Wisdom, declared that "He that sinneth against me wrongeth his own soul: all they that hate me love death" (Prov. 8:36). This love of death and will to death is the consequence of man's apostasy from God. As God said to Israel, "O Israel, thou hast destroyed thyself; but in me is thine help" (Hos. 13:9). Man brings judgment and death on himself by his apostasy. Sinners, according to St. Paul, are "Backbiters, haters of God, despiteful, proud, boasters, inventors of evil things, disobedient to parents, Without understanding, covenant breakers, without natural affection, implacable, unmerciful; Who knowing the judgment of God, that they which commit such things are worthy of death, not only do the same, but have pleasure in them that do them" (Rom. 1:30–32).

The only antidote to this will to death is Jesus Christ, who declared, "I am the resurrection, and the life" (John 11:25), in whoms alone we have newness of life and the will to live. In Him, our being, from its innermost wellsprings, is governed by life, and the righteousness and resurrection of Jesus Christ. The will to death is then broken, and the will to live given direction.

Scripture Index

Index

The Author

Rousas John Rushdoony (1916-2001) was a well-known American scholar, writer, and author of over thirty books. He held B.A. and M.A. degrees from the University of California and received his theological training at the Pacific School of Religion. An ordained minister, he worked as a missionary among Paiute and Shoshone Indians as well as a pastor to two California churches. He founded the Chalcedon Foundation, an educational organization devoted to research, publishing, and cogent communication of a distinctively Christian scholarship to the world-at-large. His writing in the *Chalcedon Report* and his numerous books spawned a generation of believers active in reconstructing the world to the glory of Jesus Christ. Until his death, he resided in Vallecito, California, where he engaged in research, lecturing, and assisting others in developing programs to put the Christian Faith into action.

The Ministry of Chalcedon

CHALCEDON (kal-see-don) is a Christian educational organization devoted exclusively to research, publishing, and cogent communication of a distinctively Christian scholarship to the world at large. It makes available a variety of services and programs, all geared to the needs of interested ministers, scholars, and laymen who understand the propositions that Jesus Christ speaks to the mind as well as the heart, and that His claims extend beyond the narrow confines of the various institutional churches. We exist in order to support the efforts of all orthodox denominations and churches. Chalcedon derives its name from the great ecclesiastical Council of Chalcedon (AD 451), which produced the crucial Christological definition: "Therefore, following the holy Fathers, we all with one accord teach men to acknowledge one and the same Son, our Lord Jesus Christ, at once complete in Godhead and complete in manhood, truly God and truly man...." This formula directly challenges every false claim of divinity by any human institution: state, church, cult, school, or human assembly. Christ alone is both God and man, the unique link between heaven and earth. All human power is therefore derivative: Christ alone can announce that, "All power is given unto me in heaven and in earth" (Matthew 28:18). Historically, the Chalcedonian creed is therefore the foundation of Western liberty, for it sets limits on all authoritarian human institutions by acknowledging the validity of the claims of the One who is the source of true human freedom (Galatians 5:1).

The Chalcedon Foundation publishes books under its own name and that of Ross House Books. It produces a magazine, *Faith for All of Life,* and a newsletter, The *Chalcedon Report,* both bimonthly. All gifts to Chalcedon are tax deductible. For complimentary trial subscriptions, or information on other book titles, please contact:

Chalcedon
Box 158
Vallecito, CA 95251 USA
(209) 736-4365
www.chalcedon.edu